DON'T TEXT THAT MAN!

A Guide to Self- Protective

Dating In The Age Of Technology

RHONDA FINDLING

The front cover is a replication of the image of the painting "Love" painted by Xhovalin Delia

ALSO BY RHONDA FINDLING

Table of Contents

PART 2

INTRODUCTION

When I wrote *Don't Call That Man!* more than a decade ago, there were only three ways to contact a man you had broken up with or who had broken up with you. Either you'd call him on the telephone, see him in person, or you could write him a letter, put a stamp on it and mail it. Today's technology has totally changed the world of relationships.

Although the internet has enormously transformed our lives for the better it has also become an alluring irresistible playground and gathering place for psychologically challenged men who may be socially inappropriate, mentally injurious, sexually challenged, psychiatrically ill, character disordered, and generally messed up. A woman's time and energy can be wasted by email bantering or texting with a man who can vanish, then reappear with ease by assuming aliases and nicknames.

Even men with the most minimal social skills, who couldn't get a date in high school, can attract a woman on his Facebook page with an illusion he's created. He can seduce with texts equivalent to great poetry while having simultaneous flirtations with multiple women.

Some men have told me that women are more dispensable than ever. It's as if they're "in a candy store". These men declared that they don't even have to bother working on relationship issues with women they're involved with because, if things don't work out, there's always another available woman they can meet on a dating website or Facebook.

The relationship books of our recent past just don't apply anymore. *The Rules* warned women about fantasy relationships. However, fantasy relationships are so common now. Provocative, electronic, sexualized behavior with non-physicality is running rampant. It's currently very popular to have flirty cyber relationships online and never even talk on the phone or meet in person.

Books like *He's Just Not That Into You*, which was widely promoted and championed by media and talk shows, do not help out the situation. It's an insult to women traumatized by men who chased, seduced and even proclaimed their love, to ultimately have a bait and switch pulled on them. The rules and explanations from these simplistic books don't take into account the multidimensional forces and dynamics that take place in relationships between men and women in our current culture. Nor do they acknowledge the large body of psychological work and psychoanalytic literature written about relationships by some of the most brilliant clinicians of the past century.

Let me say right here as a psychotherapist, who's clocked in thousands of clinical hours treating both men and women, that there are many men who are very much "into a woman" but have some part of them that prevents them from attaching. They have a compelling need to sabotage and destroy connections with women as they become closer and their relationships start to deepen.

I'd like to clarify that the men with intimacy problems I will psychologically explore in this book are not monsters and psychopaths out to harass you, murder, kidnap your children or take your life savings. This is not a book about men right out of a Lifetime TV movie. *Don't Text That Man!* is about men who are human but have attachment issues and severe problems with intimacy. I am writing about men we fall in love with and then unfortunately have to get away from to emotionally survive. Men, who can be amazing and even loving, but have an inability to form stable and satisfying relationships.

Don't Text That Man! is not about technology. *Don't Text That Man!* is a psychological examination of men now armed with technology as tools and defenses to hide behind, enabling them to relate to women in even more limited, immature dysfunctional ways than ever before.

Don't Text That Man! is based on my psychotherapeutic work and communication with thousands of clients and readers of my books from all over the world. I have also attended conferences on love, sexuality and relationships throughout the US and Europe where I listened and spoke to the most prolific psychoanalysts and behavior theorists of our time. I have recently started to present my own workshops on my clinical work at these conferences.

Don't Text That Man! will validate and explain many of your demoralizing, traumatic experiences with men. It will transport you out of the victim position. *Don't Text That Man!* will empower you by offering more insight into men to determine if a man, you are interested in or involved with, has the emotional capacity to sustain a grownup, mature, viable relationship. It will help you prevent yourself from getting hurt or, at the very least, minimize the odds.

I describe the signs, behavior and traits of Malignant Men so you don't take their behaviors so personally and get too deeply wounded. You will be able to separate which is about you and what is it about him and his issues. It will help you determine when you should fight for a relationship with a man and when you should walk away. *Don't Text That Man!* will also help you try to relate in a healthier way to Malignant Men if you do decide to try to work it out with him. You will also learn how to deal with feelings and thoughts that might be causing you to act self-destructively with men.

The second part of *Don't Text That Man!* will help you detach from a man you've determined is emotionally unhealthy, depleting and destructive. *Don't Text That Man!* will also help you learn to cope with ruminating, obsessive thinking and feelings of aggression towards a man who may have hurt you.

I don't believe in the concept of "next' as a form of coping. Men are not interchangeable objects. If you love and adore a man (despite his pathology), it can be very hard to quickly find another man to replace him. Maybe some women are lucky enough to detach instantly and find a new love so fast. However, being unable to find a new relationship can bring further frustration, shame and feelings of inadequacy and deprivation on top of the loss you are already struggling with.

Even with all the social and economical advances women have made, deep down most women still long for love from a man. It's part of the human condition. However, due to the new technological world we are living in, women truly need to be smarter and more self-protective than ever before. It can be done. *Don't Text That Man!* will teach you how.

Part I

ONE

Malignant Men

If you've ever been left feeling broken, hurt, injured and/or traumatized by a man, then you've had an involvement with a Malignant Man.

If you've ever had a connection with a man who totally confused you with double messages, then you've been with a Malignant Man.

If you've ever known a man who was the sweetest nicest guy in the whole world but ended up sabotaging or destroying the connection once you tried to bump it up a notch, then you've had an encounter with a Malignant Man.

How Do Malignant Men Sabotage Relationships?

By saying or doing something that ruins your relationship. They can be insulting, rejecting, devaluing, cruel, mean, spiteful, controlling, aggressive, impatient, negligent, emotionally absent, indifferent, rejecting, deceitful, frustrating, sadistic or hurtful. Sometimes they just disappear. They have the capacity to get you to desire them and then push you to the breaking point. It's an encounter with a Malignant Man that usually brings women to my office or call me for a phone consultation.

Many Malignant Men have tremendous anxiety about women. A Malignant Man might be afraid of being invaded, pursued, punished, engulfed, attacked, destroyed, consumed, upset, irritated and/or intruded upon by a woman. At the very worst Malignant Men see women as castrating, sexually ravenous, manipulative and power hungry. Sometimes Malignant Men are afraid they will be forced to do what they do not want to do as if they have no boundaries. A telltale sign of a Malignant Man — he is usually unaware of, in denial of, or just won't acknowledge his relationally destructive behavior, no matter how unhappy he is or his obvious lack of successful relationships. He is usually locked into his own subjective reality and often finds any feedback on his way of thinking about relationships as a personal attack. He prevents real contact from being made by using various methods of distancing and evasion, which I will explore in more detail later.

A woman doesn't have to do anything to trigger his intimacy problems. In fact, the more normal a woman acts in terms of attaching, the more a Malignant Man's pathology may get activated.

Malignant Men are not "all bad". In fact they can be wonderful. Even amazing. That's why we're drawn to them. That's why we fall in love with them. They can be irresistible, interesting, talented, brilliant, captivating, sexy, attentive, engaging, fun, promising, sweet, supportive, lovable, paternal and loving. The tragedy is that these healthy characteristics are only parts of them. It's when you get close and more intimately involved (not necessarily sexually) with Malignant Men their destructive, hurtful behavior becomes activated.

Claire Bloom's description of her ex-husband, the famous author Phillip Roth, in her memoir *Leaving A Doll's House* beautifully captures the essence of a Malignant Man:

"And Philip played that elusive role — one moment an understanding, thoughtful, compassionate, surrogate parent and next a remote, unyielding, punishing adversary."

Signs Of A Malignant Man

The following are descriptions of Malignant Men's behaviors. One behavior trait could be a sign to be careful. Two behavior traits — he's probably a Malignant Man. Three behavior traits — you're dealing with a bonafide Malignant Man:

Limited Empathy For Others
He has a difficult time understanding how you feel. He doesn't seem to have the capacity or tools to have empathy for others.

Doesn't Like When You Get Angry At Him

If you get confrontational with him, you are history. You have to stay calm even if you're enraged.

Doesn't Like Demands Made On Him

He experiences requests to meet your needs as demands or intrusive. You feel as if you are walking on eggshells when you ask him to do anything.

Doesn't Like To Be Held Accountable

He finds it difficult to take ownership of his behavior. He will do anything to justify his actions rather than admit he was wrong. Even if it means losing the relationship.

Tendency To Idealize And Devalue

First you're his fantasy woman. Eventually you do something to disappoint him or he finds something imperfect about you and you're thrown off the pedestal.

Plays Warped Psychological Games

Sometimes he plays twisted psychological games, which provide interaction and drama, but are a poor substitute for intimacy.

His "Self" Always Comes First

His primary focus is on his "self". Love and relationships are always secondary, even if he proclaims differently. He's stuck in his interior world.

Sends You Double Messages

He runs hot and cold. Sometimes he makes you feel like you are going crazy. Push-pull, appear-disappear-reappear, I love you; I can't stand to be with you.

Has Problems With Closeness And Distance

He creates obstacles to bonding. He may be the guy engaging you on the internet but never wants to meet. Technology now offers many ways of communicating without intimacy, which exacerbates this problem.

Doesn't Try And Repair Or Restore When Things Go Wrong

If you have an argument or altercation, he seals off into his own world and doesn't make an attempt to repair or restore the relationship. Often he doesn't have the relationship skills to try and fix it.

He's Smug Or Arrogant

His smugness is off the chart. His arrogance has nothing to do with being financially or professionally successful though. He can be poor as a church mouse and still think he's "all that".

He's Unpredictable

You never know what's up with him. He's exciting, never boring but very depleting and upsetting. He switches his personality at the drop of a hat.

Entitled
He may be obese, bald, unemployed and on disability but he feels he deserves a woman with Hollywood looks or is thirty years younger than him. He doesn't appreciate what he had or is being offered.

Limited Self Awareness
He's not aware of how he sabotages his own success. He has poor insight into himself. He is often in heavy denial, refusing to look at his dysfunctional behavior.

Wants To Be Mysterious
Wanting to be known is avoided and real relating is obviated. It's easy to fall in love with a man who's mysterious because you build him up into a fantasy and idealize him.

Very Defensive
He hides behind his psychological defenses. He chooses aggressive self-protection over vulnerability and authenticity.

Frustrating
He can be very frustrating. His needs will always come before your needs.

Immature
Everything has to be his way. He might even throw a tantrum!

Complicated
You often find yourself processing his behavior and your relationship with people in your support system. Often you feel like his therapist. He's difficult to please.

He "gaslights" You
He tries to get you to doubt your reality. This emotionally abusive dynamic is commonly known in the pop psychology/recovery world as "gaslighting" and refers to the classic 1944 film *Gaslight*, where a wife, eager for her abusive husband's approval, believes his reality over hers until she starts to lose her mind.

He Can Act Outrageously Obnoxious
He can be combative, argumentative, critical, offensive, rude, dismissive and/or
know-it-all.

He Can Detach At The Drop Of A Hat
He shuts down when he's upset, overwhelmed or afraid of intimacy. He stops relating even though you're in the same room.

He Tries To Make You Jealous And Then Blames It On You
He comments on women's body parts. He compares you to other women. He'll tell you whom he's attracted to.

He's Undependable

He lies. He doesn't follow through on what he tells you. He doesn't call when he says he will. He cancels on you.

Feelings A Malignant Man May Induce In You

The following are the feelings you may experience when you're relating to a Malignant Man:

Hurt
Mad
Abandoned
Worthless
Traumatized
Deprived
Frustrated
Denigrated
Ignored
Harmed
Bewildered
Exhausted
Miserable
Confused
Left
Devastated
Stuck
Dismissed

Alone
Lonely
Haunted
Cut off
Used
Played
Fooled
Humiliated
Ridiculed
Devalued
Scared
Insulted
Want to cry
Not heard
Not understood
Unwanted
Undesired
Betrayed
Rejected
Ignored
Sexually used
Sexually objectified
Sexually undesired
Unsafe
Bad about yourself
You want to get away from him
Depleted
Angry
Violated

Upset
Stressed out
Inadequate
Invalidated
Discounted
Duped
Manipulated
Demoralized
Destroyed
Attacked
Driven crazy
Tortured
Unloved
Disliked
Enraged
Sadistic
Unattractive
Unappreciated
Hopeless

TWO

The Classic Malignant Man Prototypes

The following are classic prototypes of Malignant Men. Please remember that all of the prototypes intertwine and overlap. Most Malignant Men don't fall under one specific category but are a combination of traits.

Mr. Hook Up Guy

You'll have a great sexual experience with him and then he unconsciously spoils it by devaluing you or never calling you again, leaving you feeling used or even played. He experiences a triumphant contempt for women after seducing and then dropping them. Often he sees more than one woman at a time.

He gets disappointed and angry when a woman expresses her needs or, God forbid, demands a relationship or commitment after being sexual. He makes you feel like a sexual object because he's not relating to you as a whole person.

Mr. Prince Of Darkness

The pouty brooding Marlon Brandos. The Heathcliff (for those who have read *Wuthering Heights*). He's a combination of angry, gothic, vindictive, shadowy, tantalizing, captivating and even cruel. Sometimes, within minutes of being fun-loving, he becomes dark, moody, sullen and angry. His mood is like black ink that permeates everything surrounding him. You feel as if you are walking on broken glass.

Unfortunately, he is talented at eliciting sexual desire from women, which has absolutely nothing to do with his ability or desire to gratify them. Although his "intensity" can appear romantic, erotic, stimulating and edgy — it's sometimes "emotional disturbance" or even "psychosis". Sadly, he takes some enjoyment in suffering and you have to suffer too if you get involved with him.

Mr. Fetishist

He's only into "types", a specific kind of body type, a specific ethnicity, a specific image. He can't feel attraction for any women outside his "type". Not necessarily a beautiful image, just a particular look that he's fixated on — it could even be an unattractive look to someone else. He usually has a lot of anxiety about women who don't fall into his "type". A man like this is usually lonely because it's hard to meet women who match his very specific criteria.

Mr. Superficial

He's mostly into looks and body parts rather than looking at women as a whole person. He only values women who are young and highly attractive. He doesn't care much about substance, intellect, character, talent, intelligence and a great sense of humor. If you're over thirty and don't looks like a playboy centerfold or movie star you're out of commission.

There are men who pay matchmakers over thirty thousand dollars a shot just to meet "model" looking women. However if you are blessed with good "beauty genes", God help you if something happens to your looks as you age, because he will drop you in a heartbeat.

Mr. De-valuer

He wants (or proclaims to want) to fall in love. However, he crosses women off the list who are not perfect enough for him. He's waiting for his ideal woman. He dates and dates always finding fault with women who are available, devaluing women who are interested in him. I've actually heard men say they can't commit to a woman because she was "allergic to wheat", "her hands are too big", "had hammertoes", and "she couldn't bicycle as far as him". He can be the biggest loser in the world but he still feels entitled to his fantasy woman.

Mr. Masochist

He's into women who are rejecting, frustrating, tantalizing or otherwise unavailable. He prefers longing for a woman rather than relating to her in a real, authentic relationship. Although he's masochistic he will sometimes act sadistic to women who are available and desire him.

Mr. Stuck in the Past

He carries a torch for an old girlfriend(s). He hasn't seen her in years but still thinks of her all the time and hopes she'll come back to him. He's always in a state of frustration or longing for woman from his past. This is both masochistic and a way to avoid a real, viable relationship.

Mr. Mystery Man

He can't really become intimate with a woman because he doesn't want to "be known". He doesn't reveal much, so you can "idealize him". It's easy to fall in love with a man who's mysterious because you build him up into a fantasy since you don't really know who he is. Mystery men are often cryptic and you have to read into their behavior and what they tell you.

Mr. Attached Man

Some attached men (this includes married men) like the dynamic of having two women in their lives who may even fight over him. He enjoys frustrating one or both of them. He manages two relationships by compartmentalizing.

Mr. Therapist

This type of Malignant Man uses listening, empathy and psychological support to attempt to seduce and engage women. Occasionally he can be some type of mental health practitioner or is studying to become a therapist. He is spiritual or claims to be, often using New Age concepts as his calling card. These types of men are usually attracted to women who are not that interested in them or unavailable because they are attached to someone else, have emotional problems, or are too young. When these men have the opportunity for a viable relationship with an emotionally available woman, who truly wants them or is attracted to them, they run in the other direction.

THREE

The Sexually Ambivalent Man

The Malignant Man Who Doesn't Have Sex Or Withholds Sex

As a former 1980's disco queen and nightclub girl, my experience with men who had intimacy issues was they wanted sex but with no strings attached. However, as technology has advanced, I've been hearing more stories about men acting seductive and then not wanting sex!

An experience with a man like this can be totally traumatizing because he makes you feel bad about yourself as a woman — as if there's something wrong with you.

In person, he'll flirt, gaze and even touch — giving a woman the impression that he's romantically interested. Technologically, he woos women using texting, socialization sites (Facebook, etc.) and emailing. But he never acts on his seductive behavior. He's all blah blah blah and no cha cha cha. He may have a desire to be with a woman for emotional connection but not for sex.

If a woman finally makes a move on a Sexually Ambivalent Man he'll look at her as if she's nuts, throwing his hands up in panic pleading, "Oh no! Just friends!" He'll tell her or insinuate that all this romantic stuff is in her head. Her imagination. How dare she even think for a moment that he'd be romantically interested in her?

If a woman confronts him about his mixed signals, he'll only justify his behavior. He will never own his ambivalence. He'll put it all on you. He'd rather lose the friendship/connection then admit he's been leading you on.

One of my pet peeves is people who think that a woman is into a "fantasy" relationship when a man has sent her "double messages". Very rarely have I met or treated a woman who had a fantasy relationship where it is all in her head. Almost all of the time, the relationship is mutual. This type of confusing situation is often caused by a man who induces romantic feelings in her and then doesn't follow through. A Sexually Ambivalent Man can make a woman feel like she is going crazy!

Why We Like Them

It's easy to fall for a Sexually Ambivalent Man because he makes you feel safe. He doesn't push sex on you. He knows how to keep it in his pants. Unfortunately, he never wants to take it out of his pants!

Women, burnt out from men who are overly focused on sex, can easily fall prey to a Sexually Ambivalent Man because he gives them time to develop a connection. They think he's being a gentleman and is more interested in getting to know them as a person. A Sexually Ambivalent Man is ultimately emotionally dangerous because he makes his victims feel unloved, undesired, humiliated, inadequate, ugly, repulsive, rejected, deeply hurt and traumatized.

Sexual Problems

Sometimes a viable sexual problem is the culprit behind a Sexually Ambivalent Man's conflicted behavior. I've listed physical and medical causes why a man would deprive himself of sex with a woman he feels connected to. The following symptoms can also be applied to men who are sexual and then lose all interest in having sex:

- He has an STD he doesn't want you to know about
- He's impotent (erectile dysfunction)
- He has premature ejaculation and doesn't want you to know
- He cannot sustain an erection if he uses a condom
- He has OCD (a germ phobia)
- He takes anti-depressants which sometimes create lack of sexual desire, impotence and can jeopardize feelings of romantic love and attachment
- He has something physically wrong with him (anemic, diabetic, hypothyroidism, Parkinson's disease, cardiovascular disease)
- He has lack of sexual desire in general
- He's terrified sexually transmitted diseases can be fatal
- He has rapid ejaculation
- He has Anorgasmia (lack of orgasmic fulfillment)
- He has performance anxiety
- He has low sexual self-esteem
- He takes antihypertensive medications
- He takes tranquilizers

- He has chronic pain
- He suffers from andropause
- He drinks too much alcohol
- He doesn't have enough testosterone in the body

Emotional Reasons

The following are emotional reasons why a man engages a woman in some type of relationship but does not want to be sexual with her:

Denial of Homosexuality

I believe that many Sexually Ambivalent Men are in denial of their homosexuality. They know they're gay and may have even acted out homosexual feelings but are hoping they will eventually meet the right woman who will create the desire they are searching for. They may keep dating and dating and never have a real relationship. They enjoy the company of women and their companionship, however they're just not sexually attracted to women.

They may have a lot of shame and choose to live in a state of denial. When their woman friend wants more, they'll tell her that they're not attracted to her or just want to be friends. The woman ends up feeling frustrated and insulted, which usually results in the demise of the friendship.

Internet Porn

Men who are afraid of intimacy or relationships can now fulfill their sexual needs by watching internet pornography. Some men are so into isolated fantasy they can't even feel sexual desire for real women anymore because they don't match up to the images of women on the computer screen.

I once had a patient who said that he preferred pornography to a real woman. He claimed that he didn't want to have to deal with another person, which he considered stressful rather than gratifying.

Into Prostitutes

He feels comfortable having sex with a "live" woman but someone he does not have an emotional relationship with. If he pays her and is detached from his feelings he is able to function sexually, with minimum anxiety or trauma.

Mental Illness

He may have mental health issues that make him flee intimacy such as schizophrenia, a very deep clinical depression or a schizoid personality disorder. If he is hearing voices or is paranoid, he may fear being sexual. Men who are schizophrenic often don't like sex.

Sexual Abuse

Some men are terrified of sex because they were sexually abused as children. They long for intimacy but have a deep fear or dread of sex.

Early physical or sexual abuse may have numbed their emotions and disconnected them from human warmth, interaction and trust.

Sexual Anorexia

In Patrick Carnes' book *Sexual Anorexia*, he claims that sexual anorexia is an obsessive state in which the physical, mental and emotional task of avoiding sex dominates one's life. Like self-starvation with food, compulsive hoarding or debating, sex becomes an enemy to be continually denied. Deprivation of sex can also make him feel more in control and protect him against all chances of getting hurt. He may also get some masochistic gratification out of depriving himself of sex.

Humiliation

Some men have a fear of being rejected, ridiculed and humiliated by women. They may even become impotent as an expression of this fear. They're afraid the woman will devalue them if they don't perform to her standards. They may reject women sexually so they don't have to disclose their impotence. They would forgo the gratification of a sexual experience rather than a woman's critical observation. Their fear of women may also lead to revulsion of women sexually.

Fear of Intimacy

With sexual intimacy comes further emotional intimacy. A man who is terrified of closeness may choose to deprive himself of a sexual experience with a woman he already has a connection with, who is romantically interested in him.

If his fear of intimacy is so powerful, a Sexually Ambivalent Man will do what he has too to push her away, to stop the pressure. He may even imply that something is wrong with her. She is deficient, inadequate, not his type. He'll even tell her that he just wants to be friends and was never attracted to her, just to get rid of her. He can even become nasty and insulting. These are both conscious and unconscious distancing strategies.

Overwhelmed By Emotions

Some men can get so overwhelmed with anxiety, anger, rage, hostility or fear of loss of self that their sexual desire completely diminishes. They start out feeling an attraction towards a woman and then talk themselves out of it. They split off from their erotic feelings.

Poor Sense of Self

Some men are so scared of the "loss of self" that they lose all sense of romantic feelings or sexual desire. When you don't have a strong "sense of self" you can feel intruded upon by others when they try to get close to you. The fear of connection makes a Malignant Man distance and cut his feelings off. This could be caused by having an inadequate or traumatizing childhood.

Power and Control

He's more interested in the conquest and seduction (knowing he can have her) than sex. He also may enjoy having the power of withholding sex so he can control a woman in order to protect his vulnerability.

Perversions
Straight sex or a woman's naked body just won't do it for him. He has fetishes and perversions, which are the only way he can feel sexual excitement and desire.

Dealing With the Sexually Ambivalent Man

The most distinctive trait of the Sexually Ambivalent Man is his lack of ownership of the mixed messages he sends. He does not hold himself accountable for his behavior even though he witnesses the destruction of his relationships with women.

A healthy, single unattached man, who is not sexually interested in you, doesn't act seductively unless he can back it up. Most men don't tease. When they act seductively they usually mean business.

A man depriving himself of having sex with a woman, who is sexually interested in him, with whom he has some type of friendship or relationship, is demonstrating atypical behavior. There's usually something just not right about "that man"!

FOUR

The Severely Emotionally Avoidant Malignant Man

The Severely Emotionally Avoidant Man has a severe terror of closeness. Out of all the Malignant Men I have mentioned, he has the greatest difficulty connecting due to his compulsive need to detach when he feels himself getting too close to a woman.

A Severely Emotionally Avoidant Man is confusing because he can be very engaging and sociable. In fact, his ability to connect is almost tantalizing and what tricks you into falling for him. He has developed certain ways of behaving to bring people into his life, while at the same time, remaining emotionally withdrawn and hidden in a safe place in his own internal world.

His emotionally avoidant features become more apparent once you start to get to know him better. Unfortunately, this often happens after you've already started to get attached to him. If a Severely Emotionally Avoidant Man does manage to find himself getting into some form of a relationship or intimate situation, he will end up feeling pressured or manipulated. He will unconsciously figure out how to distance himself and get out of the situation. Even a platonic friendship with a woman could be threatening if it starts to get too intense, possibly leading to romance and sex.

The Severely Emotionally Avoidant Man has an amazing ability to mobilize avoidance maneuvers at a moment's notice. When he's in distancing mode, this man can be completely insensitive — often appearing cynical, cold, callus and devoid of emotions all together.

A Severely Emotionally Avoidant Man can also act smug and arrogant. However, his superior behavior is not about narcissistic grandiosity but more like wanting to be at a distance — not connected.

A Severely Emotionally Avoidant Man is usually not deliberately trying to be emotionally abusive when he's heartlessly detaching. He's just trying to find psychic safety. His retreat from human closeness is not caused by disinterest in a relationship or love but rather by his emotional fragility and fear of fragmentation.

What you may think are normal intimacy demands, he experiences as intrusive. It's not actually people he wants to avoid, but the emotions he feels as a result of intimacy. It's his desperate need to retreat into himself, which causes him to destroy possible opportunities for love and relationships.

A Severely Emotionally Avoidant Man feels more comfortable with people who make few emotional or intimate demands on him. His ongoing relationships that last are usually superficial and based on intellectual and recreational activities. He can maintain a relationship as long as there is no demand placed on him for emotional intimacy.

Often, he hasn't had a serious relationship for many years although he gets many opportunities. Sometimes he'll hold a torch for years for a woman who's unavailable and may have rejected him. Acting this way demonstrates he is relating to someone internally but not in reality.

Sexuality

Many Severely Emotionally Avoidant Men have a normal sex drive but often prefer sexual abstinence or masturbation rather the emotional closeness they must tolerate when having sex. Severely Emotionally Avoidant Men often feel that their personal space is being violated when they do have sex.

If a Severely Emotionally Avoidant Man decides he does want to have sex with a partner, he sometimes prefers a stranger, rather than a woman he's having intimate/emotional connections with, to reduce the intimacy in the sexual experience.

Relating To Him

His insensitivity, resulting from his intense need to disconnect, can evoke enormous amounts of rage and sadism in a woman. He can be lethal — making a woman feel unloved, undesired, inadequate, ugly, repulsive and rejected. Do not feed into these feelings he induces in you by retaliating. It will only justify his existing pathological thinking that he doesn't need anyone and that he should stay alone.

If you start to confront him, he'll probably remain passive and you'll get more frustrated at his indifference and detachment.

He may distort your reality and tell you why there's "no relationship" or "no feelings" on his part when you knew that there was. He needs to believe his own "story" so that he can be in denial of his own problems.

A Severely Emotionally Avoidant Man can be lethal so beware if you fall for one! If you have any prior issues of abuse, rejection or abandonment you could end up devaluing yourself and bearing the responsibility for the failures in the relationship rather than seeing his part in it.

FIVE

Why Do Malignant Men Destroy Relationships With Women?

Many Malignant Men will verbally express genuine yearnings for relationships and even marriage. Sometimes they claim that they want to fall in love. Unfortunately, Malignant Men don't have the capacity to fulfill these desires. They will do something to disrupt the potential for growth and continued attachment with a woman. They get in their own way by spoiling their own chances with warm, loving, emotionally and sexually available women that are clearly interested in them.

Defense Against Intimacy

A Malignant Man's distancing behavior is very often a defense against the experience of "intimacy". Closeness and attachment stir up many feelings for a Malignant Man: terror, severe anxiety, abandonment, hurt, rejection, engulfment, and/or intrusiveness. Sometimes they have been deeply hurt in the past. Their terror of being wounded again causes them to resist opportunities for intimacy.

Interestingly enough, Malignant Men bring on the very state of anxiety, abandonment and disappointment that they were unconsciously trying to prevent and defend themselves from. Ultimately distancing behavior feels "safer" because they don't feel as vulnerable but it eventually brings about anxiety and even worse conditions for them — loneliness and rejection. In fact, a Malignant Man's fear of being left can lead to a self-fulfilling prophecy. Ironically, by not allowing intimacy he sets himself up for the possibility of being left by a woman.

Acts Sadistic

Sadism is sometimes present in situations where women feel rejected, abandoned or played by a man. A Malignant Man who is sadistic can be withholding in a subtly cruel and tormenting fashion. He finds depriving a woman who wants or needs something from him (sex, emotional support) exciting. Frustrating, disappointing, rejecting and even humiliating a woman can feel a lot more gratifying than having a "real" authentic relationship with her.

Often Malignant Men, who act sadistic, may not even be aware of their own sadism. It's not until they've been rejected by many women for their destructive behavior that they start to finally get it. The following are maladaptive ways that Malignant Men relate when sadism is prominent:

- He finds frustrating women gratifying
- He finds seducing women and then dropping them gratifying
- He finds disappointing women gratifying

- Recognition of his damaging, hurtful effects on women are nonexistent
- He sets women up to reject, hurt or humiliate him (which is also masochistic)

In addition to being addicted to the excitement he gets from being sadistic, there are some other reasons for his cruelty:

- The woman becomes a symbol of everything that's wrong in his life
- He feels validated by having an impact on a woman through hurting her, which makes his poor sense of self feel better
- Sadistic behavior is a coping strategy to assert control over his life and to re-establish his superiority over women (misogyny)
- He wants to rid himself of his own self-loathing by placing it onto someone else. If a woman likes him, he devalues her because she reminds him of his own vulnerable self and needs to put her down to release his own rage and self-hatred. The more vulnerable the woman, the greater his contempt.

If you can understand that some Malignant Men have very sadistic feelings toward women, you won't personalize the awful ways they can behave towards you. You will understand that it is about them and not you. However, if you choose to continue a relationship with a man you realize is sadistic, then you are allowing yourself to take part in a sadomasochistic relationship.

Seeks Retribution

Sometimes a Malignant Man's primary interest is in retribution — not love. He may have been deeply hurt by a woman or many women (mother, female family members, past girlfriends, wives). He never worked through the loss by mourning and grieving the relationship(s) with the woman who hurt him, which would open up a psychic space for him to become emotionally available to love again. Instead, he retaliates by rejecting or humiliating a woman if she makes herself vulnerable to him by liking/loving him. It might not be the original woman who hurt him, but it's the next best thing.

Sometimes his feelings of anger and contempt from the past are channeled into hatred rather than love and sexuality. This type of emotional integration can result in his acting sadistic or abusive to a woman as well as feeling impotent and/or sexually disinterested.

Envious

A Malignant Man may be tremendously envious of a woman. He may feel she is more successful, better-looking, happier, earns more money, has the ability to love and/or have a relationship, more talented, and has the ability to feel. The list is endless. It could be something that neither you nor he is even aware of. Some Malignant Men's envy is very primitive and comes from a very young place.

Envy can be deeply destructive and spoiling. Sadly, a Malignant Man who acts out his envy also destroys his own chance for a connection — a woman he could find love with. His envy could evoke aggressive feelings towards a woman, resulting in his emotionally hurting or insulting her. In fact, devaluation is a common and effective defense against envy. If what you have is worthless, I could not possibly envy it.

Difficulties With Mentalization

There are now studies of the process of metallization, which is a form of mental activity or mental functioning that deals with relating to other people and forming attachments. The activation of the attachment system simultaneously deactivates many brain centers associated with forming close relationships, which would cause a man to act destructively when trying to develop a relationship with a woman.

Very Immature

Some Malignant Men are just very immature. They are developmentally arrested at a young age. It's like being involved with a boy in men's clothing. They can seem very adult in certain areas of their life but, when it comes to relationships, it's like you're dealing with an eight year old.

For instance, when preteen boys feel anxious with their female therapist, they may make devaluing comments about her. She's ugly, she smells, her room is yucky.

To use Freudian analytic jargon, they're at the latency stage. Did you ever see "The Little Rascals" or "Dennis the Menace"? They think girls have cooties. They're at the *I still don't like girls* stage; sometimes they don't even want sex!

Sabotages Relationships

Some Malignant Men are masochistic and feel they don't deserve love so they destroy any real opportunities of connection. Their loyalties to their mother or father, who abused or injured them, may also be reenacted by sabotaging themselves. They feel compelled to spoil and waste their opportunities with available women.

Makes Poor Choices of Women To Attach To

Some men desire healthy emotional connections with women but can only feel romantic desire for unavailable women (women who are in other relationships or who just don't reciprocate their interest). These men truly suffer because they can't seem to fall in love with women who really want them. They can provoke women they have connections with to end relationships with them

45

usually due to their own lack of romantic interest. Eventually, the women find them to be insulting, frustrating and unbearable to endure or tolerate. Sometimes Malignant Men end the relationship due to their inability to romantically/sexually attach to a healthy, available woman.

SIX

Malignant Men's Most Popular Psychological Defense

The most popular psychological defense a Malignant Man often utilizes when he's relating to women is projective identification.

Projective identification is when a person disowns and discharges a feeling that is painful or uncomfortable and stimulates it in another person. The other person's mind then becomes the container to accept and understand the unwanted projected feelings. It's as if you are a blank movie screen and your Malignant Man is the projector. The film is whatever is going on in his inner world.

Another way to look at projective identification is that it's a way for the two of you to be fused because you know what he's feeling. Unfortunately, his intention is not to become more intimate and romantic. In fact, projective identification reduces the sustainability of a relationship and blocks intimacy since there is no authentic relating. He just wants to expel his feelings and get rid of them because they're too much for him to bear. It is also a way for him to discharge anger and depression.

Here are some examples of the use of projective identification:

If a man feels rejected by one woman and wants to project his feelings of rejection and humiliation onto another woman (to rid himself of these intolerable feelings), he will unconsciously set up a situation where the second woman ends up feeling rejected and humiliated. Maybe he'll just tell her he doesn't want to make a commitment even though he gave her the impression he did.

If he feels jerked around by one woman, he'll break dates and reschedule a second woman and she ends up feeling jerked around. Thus he's inducing the feeling he gets from the first woman onto the second woman.

If a Malignant Man's mother was both seductive and rejecting, he may reenact the same behavior with women — making him the tantalizing, frustrating man who is just beyond reach.

If a man is anxious about his sexual performance, he could say he's not attracted to you thus projecting his feelings of inadequacy onto you by trying to make you feel like the inadequate one.

Another part of the process of projecting is known as "splitting". When people are overwhelmed with feelings they may "split off" from their emotions, which results in their being out of contact with their "feelings" and their "selves".

As a result they "act out" their feelings rather than feel, experience, express or work through them. For instance, if men feel "needy", they split off from their feelings of vulnerability and act smug and distant.

If you are very sensitive, you may be vulnerable to Malignant Men's projections and buy into them rather than seeing through their issues and defenses. This happens more often when their projections match your own issues. However, some Malignant Men might project such powerful and primitive feelings that you can still feel deeply affected by them even if you don't have a matching issue.

Some Malignant Men develop excellent radar to search out a woman with a negative self-image so that she will buy into their projections rather than realize their weaknesses.

Projections projected onto you can be very intense and difficult to resolve. It can take a very long time of arduous psychological effort and therapy to work through and shake off because they can trigger core issues. They could even make you think you're defective in some way.

It's often a result of a Malignant Man's projections that women have come to me for consultations.

SEVEN

How Did He Get Like This?

Most people are exposed to some sort of relational trauma during their childhood, which shapes their capacity for intimacy and interpersonal relationships. Just the developmental task of separating from one's mother or caretaker can take a toll.

However, it doesn't always have to be a major dramatic trauma. The family could have related in some type of dysfunctional way that wasn't conducive to his emotional growth and psychosexual maturity. He didn't have a parent or family member who was attuned to him.

As quoted in *Aggression: From Fantasy To Action:* "Even if a child has not been subject to actual violence, he will have suffered a trauma, which could be termed emotional, caused by the overall set of responses of his caregiver. Such a trauma not only leaves holes in the personality, but also affects its structure, giving rise to anxieties, arrests, and disturbances of emotional development that can lead to loss of contact with emotions".

His early relationships may have not been adapted to his needs. Perhaps he had a parent or caretaker who was depressed, in a bad marriage or not emotionally equipped to be available to him. He may have too many siblings to share Mother and Father's attention. He could have had a mentally or physically disabled sibling. Even over-gratifying a child, so he doesn't get to learn how to handle frustration, can lead to problems such as self-centeredness and narcissism.

All of these scenarios could result in a little boy feeling abandoned, rejected, unloved, neglected, intimidated and/or frightened, which affects his relationships to women as an adult.

Is It All Mommy's Fault?

Below is a list of possible dysfunctional/unhealthy ways a mother or caretaker may have related to a Malignant Man that could have deeply affected him:

- Detached
- Cold
- Abusive
- Oblivious to his emotional needs
- Neglectful
- Humiliated him
- Found him repulsive when he was a baby
- Found him sexually exciting
- Distracted with her own problems
- Controlling
- Overly possessive
- Openly attacking
- Used him as a parent to comfort herself
- Over-gratified him — gave into his every demand

Physically Absent Mother

She may have not been there for him due to emotional problems she had with closeness and attachment. She could have had a substance abuse problem, was disinterested in him, or constantly placed him in the care of others.

Emotionally Tantalizing Mother

His mother may have been depressed so she was there physically but not mentally. She wasn't attuned to his needs or psychologically connected to him. She may have distanced from him when he craved emotional closeness with her. He may have experienced her as tantalizing because he could feel her physical presence but due to her depression, he couldn't connect with the emotional part of her. As an adult he is tantalizing as well because you can feel him physically but you can't really connect with him emotionally.

Sexually Teasing Mother

He may have experienced his mother as sexually teasing and withholding when he was a young boy. This man may experience sexual desire for a woman as a repetition of early teasing by the mother, thus they unconsciously hate the desired woman. The hatred may destroy the capacity for healing, love and/or sexual excitement with a woman.

Not Emotionally Separated From Mother

Freud claims that many men never resolve their Oedipal feelings toward the mother and, as a consequence, have a psychic "splitting" between mother/friend and sexual partner. These types of men have absolutely no interest in having sex with a woman who is a friend or girlfriend. They see her as asexual even if she is very feminine and attractive. They compartmentalize their sex life, overvaluing the mother/friend as pure and sexless and, therefore, the exact opposite of a sexual woman.

Claustrophobic Mother

A Malignant Man may have had a mother who was clingy, smothering and/or needy. This type of mother can make a Malignant Man feel gobbled up by women. She also may have prevented his emotionally separating from her, resulting in his fear of being intruded upon, dominated, engulfed or manipulated. Thus when a woman gets too close to him he will possibly push her away by rejecting her or provoking her to end the relationship.

Repulsed Mother

A Malignant Man may have had a mother who found her infant's body repulsive and didn't like to touch him except when necessary. At a nonverbal level, a baby boy can pick up on his mother's disgust/dislike for his body when she is performing motherly functions such as diapering him, toilet training, picking him up when he is crying and holding him.

As a result of dysfunctional mothering a Malignant Man could be struggling with the following issues:

Hatred of Mother and/or Women

Some men have an unconscious hatred of their mother resulting in abusive, devaluing behaviors towards women. Some men express their vindictive feelings against women by degrading everything female.

Idealizes Women (Discussed In Sexually Ambivalent Man Chapter)

Some Malignant Men may idealize women whom he sees as maternal or mothers. As a result he compartmentalizes relationships with women — women he is sexual with and women who are mothers (including wives and girlfriend he desexualizes).

Ambivalence Towards Mother and/or Women

A boy's feelings towards his mother may be ambivalent: engulfed yet nurturing, seductive yet castrating. Since these feelings are repressed and pushed into the unconscious when they were young boys in order to protect the mother, Malignant Men may act out act these feelings with women as grown men.

Aggression Structured In the Psyche

If he felt rejected by his mother when he was a little boy, there may be a strong desire to injure his mother. Consequently, aggression became structured in his psyche resulting in his connecting with aggression rather than love. As a grown man he relates by hurting a woman rather than loving her.

Deficit In Mentalization

Any type of mistreatment as a child can cause a "deficit" in his metallization skills. A relationship causes anxiety, which in turn activates the attachment system and deactivates the capacity to metalize. Thus, he acts in a dysfunctional way when he attempts to attach to a woman.

EIGHT

Relating To Malignant Men

Although I am writing about men who struggle with characterological problems, not all men are hopeless. You may dating a man who you think is difficult but you feel there is hope for the relationship. If you are in such a situation, the following are some tips for trying to get along with him:

Stand In Your Truth And Reality

Maintain your own perceptions and integrity. Stand in your own sense of truth, not on what he says is true. Stay committed to your reality.

Work On Your "Self" While Relating To Him

Keep going to therapy. Talk to your friends. Go to Twelve Step programs. Your love for him should not be paramount over your love for yourself, no matter how crazy about him you are.

Stick Up For Your Needs Being Met

Be aware of your needs — emotional, financial and physical. If you're doing all the giving and your needs aren't being met, then maybe it's time to leave Dodge City.

Set And Stick To Your Boundaries

Stick to your limits! Learn to say no! If he wants to see other women, have you pay for dates, have a ménage à trios, just say "no" (if you don't want to).

Don't Be Afraid To Be Alone

Don't be afraid to be without a man. Don't hang onto him out of fear of being single. It's better to be alone and healthy then sick with someone else.

Don't Cling And Act Desperate

Don't act too needy. Desperate, clingy women make Malignant Men anxious. Try to work through your issues with your support system.

Know When To Leave The Relationship (See Next Section)

Don't wait until the relationship is completely destructive or in crisis mode to leave.

Be Aware Of Your Own Issues That Are Triggered By Malignant Men

Be aware of your own vulnerabilities. If you have traumas from your childhood you may personalize some of his behaviors towards you, which in reality may have nothing to do with you.

Is It Helpful To Act Bitchy With A Malignant Man?

I think that men, who like women who are bitchy to them, are masochistic and self-loathing. They are attracted to frustrating, withholding, and depriving women. Most likely their mothers were unavailable and frustrating to them. Love and warmth frightens them. They prefer to idealize women who are unavailable. If you're a warm woman who has the capacity to genuinely love a man, I don't think you should turn yourself into a pretzel trying to be cold and bitchy. Instead, find a man who is healthy enough to appreciate you for the warm, loving woman you are.

Why Do I Get Attracted To Malignant Men?

I don't necessarily believe that women go around finding men with relationship/attachment issues on purpose. Sometimes we meet a man, with whom we feel a genuine connection. He may be sweet and paternal. He pays attention to you. There's mutual desire.

Unfortunately, you can't always tell a man has problems until you get to know him, which means you have to spend some time with him. You may have to date him. Even have sex with him. In other words, you have to start attaching to him.

There are just no guarantees. I've known women to sleep with men on the night they've met and end up marrying them. I've known many women to wait ten dates or more to have sex with a man, only to get rejected after they finally allow themselves to let down their guard and become intimate with him. You can't always predict how things are going to turn out, which is very anxiety-inducing because you can't control everything, especially people.

Bottom line, you have to just take a chance and roll the dice. If you definitely don't want even a slight possibility of getting hurt then play it safe by never taking a risk. But then you'll never find out what you might have missed out on.

How Can I Prevent Myself From Repeatedly Getting Involved With Malignant Men?

There is no magical solution to "stop" being attracted to Malignant Men. However, if you find that you're repeatedly attracted to troubled men who don't treat you well, you may be reenacting a relationship with a parent(s) or family member who was abusive, unpredictable, rejecting or dysfunctional in some way.

You might want to see a psychotherapist to work this pattern through. You may also want to consider discussing all the men you date or are interested in with insightful, supportive, non-judgmental friends or a therapist who can help give you feedback on your choices.

Do not get angry at yourself for being attracted to Malignant Men. As I said previously, many Malignant Men can be fabulous but have intimacy/attachment problems. Just use self-discipline and will power to not continue relationships with men that you discover are Malignant Men. As the saying goes, "Keep it movin', girlfriend!" Besides, being drawn to Malignant Men are usually magnetic attractions and thankfully (or I should say hopefully) not fatal attractions.

When Is The Time To Throw In The Towel With A Malignant Man?

You may get a feeling in the pit of your stomach that tells you the relationship is unhealthy. You feel pain. You feel something awful is happening to you. You feel devastated. It's an instinct. It's in your gut.

You feel like there is a lie going on or something that is not being said. You feel helpless and stuck. You can tell he's not going to change and it's just going to be more of the same.

Here are some **specific signs** to look for to help you decide if you want to leave:

- It feels like a destructive struggle rather than a loving engagement
- You are getting emotionally hurt
- You're very depressed most of the time
- You need to go on antidepressants because of the relationship
- The relationship is unhealthy, abusive or twisted
- The relationship is intolerable
- The feelings he's inducing in you are unbearable
- He doesn't want to own his emotional problems contributing to the situation or even work on them
- Your anxiety is reaching intolerable levels
- Your integrity feels violated
- He makes you feel like you're going crazy
- Your needs aren't being met
- The pain outweighs the good things you are getting from the relationship
- You hate him and just don't want to deal with him anymore
- The relationship makes you feel mentally unwell
- Your health is affected by the stress of the relationship
- You feel depleted by the relationship
- You feel like your life is being destroyed
- He's making you act sadistic or masochistic
- You talk to your friends about him all the time, trying to figure out what to do
- You spend all your time trying to figure him out

- The relationship is interfering with your work
- You're upset all the time when you're with him
- He causes you to obsess
- You feel hopeless that he will ever meet your needs
- You feel hopeless that the relationship will ever work

Rhonda's Black Jack Theory

Know when it's time to walk away from the Black Jack table. Don't overplay your hand or else you may have a "dirty end" (pain, heartache, drama).

Don't be afraid to walk away. You may be losing him but you will also be letting go of all the pain. No more waiting. No more fantasizing. No more jealousy. No more trying to figure him out. No more frustration. No more agony. No more checking. No more obsessing. By not remaining or participating in a destructive relationship, you automatically become a healthier and self-empowered person.

Don't Second Guess Yourself

Once you make the decision to leave, don't second-guess yourself. If you try to go back, he may punish you by rejecting you. If you go back to him and he hasn't changed, you'll lose credibility. So line up with your decision.

Is There Hope For A Malignant Man If He Goes For Therapy?

Characterological change is a long, drawn-out process. So if he were to start psychotherapeutic treatment, the transformation could take a long time. He would be trying to change intrapsychic issues and interpersonal patterns. He would be trying to make a developmental shift from being "self-oriented" to "other-oriented" or bring about a greater integration of his needy dependent side with his side that is resistant to intimacy and commitment. He would be trying to work through past traumas. This could take years and that's assuming he's with a talented and highly skilled therapist.

Will Therapy Help A Malignant Man?

To break it down to specifics here are several factors that could determine a man's psychological development through therapy:

- Core internal conflicts
- How disturbed he is
- What kind of treatment he goes for
- How resistant he is
- How motivated he is to go for therapy
- Does he actually think he has a problem(s)

- How well he utilizes therapy
- How skilled and talented his therapist is
- How committed he is to change

Here are some questions to ask yourself when you're hoping he could be helped by therapy:
- Can he commit to therapy on a once a week basis
- Will he skip sessions
- Will he follow through on a long-term basis
- Is he willing he pay a therapist on an ongoing basis
- If he has commitment problems with you then there's a good chance he will have commitment problems with a therapist

Keep in mind that psychotherapy with some people is futile. Some Malignant Men are married to their pathology. Their behaviors are ego-syntonic. In other words, they think they are fine the way they are. They don't think they need to change.

Will Malignant Men Change If They Don't Go For Help?

If a man gets tired of his lifestyle filled with lack of love, isolation, failure, disconnection, pain, drama and loneliness then there's a chance he'll want to change. As some Malignant Men age, they do have regrets about their life choices.

What Eventually Happens To Malignant Men Who Don't Change?

If they don't go for treatment they usually get into the same dysfunctional situations over and over, playing the same patterns out. Malignant Men end up denying themselves love and inflict pain onto themselves when they lose out on great women who could love them. Sometimes they deteriorate and get worse. Not everyone makes it.

NINE

What To Do If You've Been Devastated By A Malignant Man

If you've just been humiliated, rejected, deeply hurt, completely devalued or traumatized by a Malignant Man, here are twelve steps to take immediately. It doesn't necessarily mean you are breaking up with him. You are just immediately getting away from him. By taking these steps, you will be taking care of yourself emotionally while keeping your self-esteem and self-respect intact.

Step One — Prepare Yourself To Leave Or Hang Up The Phone

Even though you may be in love with him or have just spent the entire weekend together, get ready to leave. If you need to, go into another room (a bathroom will do) where you can get some space from him. When you're alone, tell yourself you're going to need all the strength you have now to physically detach from him. If you're on the phone get ready to hang-up — or tell him you have to go and get off the phone.

Here are some suggestions before leaving or hanging up:

Step Two — Confront Him About His Ambivalent Behavior Or Mixed Messages

You don't want to be left feeling like a victim, so empower yourself by telling him about any of his behaviors that you experience as ambivalent, confusing, abusive, insulting and/or devaluing. There's a good chance that he's going to justify and defend his behaviors so stick with what you know and believe are rejecting, distancing, sadistic behaviors. You can also call him on his projections, double messages and his reality, if you think they're inaccurate.

If the Malignant Man is too entrenched in his pathology he will hide behind his defenses and projections to the bitter end, no matter how enlightened and on target you might sound. He'll do or say anything, even if it's insulting, degrading, devaluing and/or attacking, to justify his beliefs or words even if he knows they are a lie. Even if it means giving you up and the best sex or relationship he's ever had.

Some Malignant Men have so many defense mechanisms and projections that their reality is distorted. They may have very subjective viewpoints that may not make sense to you and certainly won't concur with your thoughts and principles.

If you feel your confrontation is getting nowhere then stop. Don't waste your time and energy if it seems hopeless. At least you'll know you tried.

Step Three — Never Go Into The Masochistic Position

Don't ever beg for love! Don't try to get him to want to be with you again, love you again, or be the way it was before he hurt you. Don't start telling him how much you love him and how you can't survive without him. Don't start asking him about other women he may be seeing. You'll regret it later. It will demoralize you and make you feel bad about yourself.

The moment that you feel you will do whatever it takes to hold onto a relationship with a man, who is hurting, rejecting or abandoning you, is when you have entered the "masochistic zone" or "masochistic position".

When you're in the masochistic position the best thing to do is detach, even if your heart feels like it is breaking into a million pieces. Shut it down girlfriend!

Surrender to his need to destroy the relationship. Let him have his free will.

Any time you spend tolerating rejecting, insulting, hurtful or traumatizing behavior is telling a man that you don't deserve better. If you want better, you have to be willing to walk. And that's true whether it's your first date or you've been married for years.

Step Four — Don't Turn Sadistic

When you're confronting him, don't say anything insulting to him even though this may feel counter intuitive. You'd probably want to say, "you're a loser", or "who the hell do you think you are anyway?" Do not verbally castrate him or cut him down to size. Then you are trying to be sadistic and put him in the masochistic position, which could lead him to being sadistic by saying something awful back to you just to get even, which may devastate you even more. Also, if there's even a part of you that thinks the relationship can be salvaged at a future time, don't say something that can never be taken back and you'll live to regret, which could lead to your contacting him compulsively to apologize.

Step Five — Don't Ask Him What's Wrong With You

Don't go into that horrible masochistic zone where you ask him specifically what's wrong with you that makes him want to reject you. Don't ask him how you can improve yourself or why he doesn't want to love you. If you start letting him criticize you and tear you apart, you will be in the masochistic position. Additionally, you will regret the information he gives you. You will only traumatize yourself even more.

So try to hold on to your self-esteem at that point even though you may feel like your guts have just fallen out.

Step Six — Don't Have Breakup Sex

Breakup sex will definitely throw you back into the masochistic position (excuse the pun). You will only feel clingier with him. There's a very good chance that you'll end up having a hysterical scene, possibly grabbing his ankles as he's walking out the door. All your defenses will be down and it will make you feel very desperate. Breakup sex may feel good while you're connected to him in the sexual act but it will feel a hundred times worse later on and you may regret it.

Step Seven — Make A Clean Exit

Just leave! Don't think of any last minute, clever, dramatic, mean things to say. If you do, you may be giving him an opening to say something back to you, which could turn into a destructive scene. Just go. Get out the door. Exit stage left. Hang up the phone if you are not with him in person.

You can fall apart once you leave but wait until you get away from him or hang up the phone. Just focus on you right now and leaving. Even though you feel like you're dying on the inside, just walk away from the relationship with your head held high.

Step Eight — Emergency Emotional Healing

Immediately call a friend or someone you can talk to about what happened so that you can vent your feelings. This will prevent you from going back to his place, turning around, texting or calling him.

If you can't get anybody on the phone then do something that will make you feel better. In other words, self-soothe. Start healing yourself. For instance, go to the gym and workout, go to a movie, go to your favorite restaurant, have a hot fudge sundae, call your therapist for an emergency appointment. Do whatever you have to, to help yourself start healing and emotionally detaching from him.

Step Nine — Don't Respond To His Texts Or Calls

Let him stew in his own anxiety and feelings of abandonment and rejection for a while. In other words, let him suffer out the consequences of his own malignant behavior. There will be plenty of time in the future that you can get back to him.

Step Ten — Plan On What To Do The Next Morning You Wake Up

The following morning can be a killer when you hit consciousness. Immediately turn on the TV or radio so that you feel connected to the world as soon as you awake. If that doesn't work, call someone to connect to (not "that man") but don't lie in your bed ruminating.

Try to put in a full day's work and stay distracted. Make an appointment for an emergency therapy session if you have to. Call people in your support system if it gets hard to get through the day.

Step Eleven — Don't Text, Email, Facebook Or Call Him

Don't contact him under any circumstances. Instead, move on to the Fifteen Step Program "Detaching From A Malignant Man" in the next chapter.

Part II

TEN

Detaching from a Malignant Man

Disengaging from a man you love, like or are infatuated with, takes a lot of self-discipline and emotional strength. It's like going against the force of gravity. It is counterintuitive. It's traumatic. It's not a natural process. It defies our human instinct to attach.

Getting over a man can take several months to several years, depending upon how attached you were to him, how much you idealized him, your childhood history, your past traumas and your opportunities to meet new men. Your feelings need to be cognitively understood, mourned, grieved and worked through.

During this time, you need to be resilient, patient and compassionate with yourself. You have to have the ability to adapt. Take as long as you need. There is no time limit. This is not a race. You must have faith and vision that you will get over him. This process does take will power and commitment. You will have to be creative, inventive and clear about your intention to detach.

Keep a Recovery Journal

Keep a recovery journal — take notes as you proceed through this journey. You will also use your journal for writing exercises at the end of the chapters. You will be able to refer to your own journal for advice and tips.

Fifteen Step Program To Detach From A Malignant Man

Here are the fifteen most important, immediate things to do to detach from a Malignant Man you've decided to end a relationship with, or who has broken up with you.

Step One — Stop All Communication With Him

Every time you communicate with him, you are sabotaging the detachment process. You are also taking the risk of getting hurt and will have to work that much harder to get over him again.

So don't call that man. Don't email that man. Don't text that man. Don't jog by that man's apartment. Don't go to nightclubs where you know that man hangs out. Don't go to some area close to his job, hoping to accidentally run into him.

Work

If you have to talk to your ex Malignant Man at work, keep it strictly about work issues. Only say hello if you feel obligated or to be professional. Don't have any social discussions with him.

Children

If you co-parent with him, only talk about children issues. Do not get into any personal discussions. Just keep it focused on the kids.

Social Events

Don't go to any parties, events or places where you know you are going to run into him. You don't need to show you're "over him" by going somewhere you know he'll turn up. You don't get a badge for suffering when you have to see him flirting with other women or a date he brought. And the worst scenario — if he doesn't respond the way you want when he sees you, you'll feel hurt all over again.

Step Two — Don't Talk To His Friends, Relatives Or Colleagues If At All Possible

Don't vent about him to people in his life. It will get back to him and inflame the situation. If you talk to his friends or relatives, there's always the possibility they could give you info that could upset you.

Step Three — Don't Ever Beg For Love

Don't grovel. Begging only makes you look pathetic, lonely and desperate. Any desire he had for you will completely disappear. Your clinging could make him feel smothered, engulfed and cause him to distance further. As I explained in the previous chapter, when you are desperately pursuing a man you have broken up with, you are putting yourself in the masochist position. You want to do whatever it takes to avoid degrading yourself.

Step Four — Build A Support System As Quickly As Possible

If you want to contact that man, call someone in your support system instead. Having a support system only helps you not to call, email or text that man but it also helps you feel understood and emotionally connected to others, which will help prevent loneliness and depression. A person in your support system will help you process your feelings so you don't act out destructively. Besides, the more you talk about what happened to you to someone in your support system, the more distance you put between yourself and the pain. Your support system could be made up of friends, family members, co-workers and professionals. Whomever you feel safe with.

- Save their phone numbers on your cell. Put them on speed dial. Memorize them or carry their numbers around.

- Have a bunch of people in your support system because you don't want to be too draining on just one person.
- Have a couple of people in your support system in different time zones so you have someone to call in the middle of the night.

Be Selective

It's important that people in your support system do not criticize or shame you. They should be emotionally supportive. It would be helpful if they are nurturing, compassionate, emotionally available, encouraging, validating and trustworthy.

The criteria for a someone in your support system is someone who:

- You feel safe with
- Can help contain your feelings
- You can process your feelings with
- Won't insult you
- Won't attack you
- Doesn't act out feelings of envy or contempt with you
- Won't project their issues onto you
- Doesn't judge you
- Doesn't give you feedback that triggers your obsessing about him

Be careful. Some people may offer you terrible advice. They could even make you feel worse. Their hurtful feedback is sometimes due to ignorance, lack of psychological mindedness, misogyny, competitiveness, envy, sadism, projective identification, emotional disturbance or just plain stupidity. If you discover that someone is not supportive, gives you bad advice or says things that make you feel worse, don' t go to them for support anymore.

Step Five — Think Before You Act Now

Don't act on impulse. Focus on the consequences of every decision you make now. This is the time to reflect on all of your behaviors. Acting on impulse can make life exciting and dramatic but it can also put you at risk because you're not thinking of the future consequences. You're just acting in the moment. Sit on your feelings. Endure your anxiety. You are in a vulnerable state of mind. Call people in your support system to discuss any impulsive urges that come over you.

Step Six — Erase All Traces Of Him From Your Environment

Throw out anything that belongs to him from your place. Mail it back to him if it's valuable. Don't use it as an excuse to call him. Anything he doesn't pick up or request, throw in the trash. If you don't want to see him, then leave it with his doorman or ask a friend to pick it up.If he lives near you consider moving. If he works near you consider changing jobs. Re-do your apartment. Get rid of anything that reminds you of him.

Step Seven — Decrease Vulnerability Physically

Take care of your body. This is not the time to go on a crash diet. See a doctor if you feel sick. Eat balanced meals. Get enough sleep. Take naps if you're not sleeping enough each night. Don't try and live on coffee even if you feel like it. Drink plenty of water. Be active and try to get some kind of exercise every day. Try not to drink or do drugs during this time. It's okay to eat comfort food now as long as it's not detrimental to your health.

Step Eight — Act "As If"

Sometimes you have to force yourself to act healthy. Even if your heart isn't in it, act "as if". Sometimes it helps to think of an archetype of a powerful woman, whether she's an actress, author or political figure. What would this archetypal woman do if she longed for a man who deeply hurt her? If it's too hard for you to not contact "that man" then imagine you are this archetypal powerful woman and "fake it till you make it".

Step Nine — Your Mental Health Comes First

Your well-being comes first! Your most important priority is to be able to function and be productive. You can't let yourself fall apart. No man is worth it. The mind can repair itself but you have to help it along by not bringing additional trauma into your life. They say that time heals all wounds but it won't work if "that man" is still present in your life. Your alliance needs to be with you and your mission to emotionally restore and repair yourself. If you find yourself crying all the time and are having difficulty functioning, then you should seek professional help.

Step Ten — Try To Understand His Pathology

Read everything you can on relationships and men. Pop psychology books, self-help books, professional psychology books, psychoanalytic books, message boards, blogs, e-books, the DSMIV. Go to conferences and workshops. There are even Psych 101 classes on YouTube now. Watch talk shows. With all the psychological information out there now, there's no need to take a man's behavior at face value. Don't be superficial. Look deeper. Empower yourself with psychological wisdom. Your newfound insight and enlightenment will help you separate his issues from yours. It will give you objectivity and distance. It will help you create a boundary so that you don't personalize his malignant behavior or accept his projections onto you.

Step Eleven — Suffering It Out — The Necessity of Mourning and Grieving

When a relationship with a man ends, you have to mourn and grieve the loss. Mourning means enduring what is. This is very difficult work. Unfortunately, there is no other way through it. No short cuts. It's very hard to do this work alone. It is often best to process your pain with someone else. Sometimes it's helpful if you can do this work with a psychotherapist. If you can't go for therapy then process your feelings with people in your support system.

You may think that the pain will never end but it does end, eventually. Be patient. Let your feelings unfold. Don't be afraid. You may think the despair will overwhelm you but it won't. During this time of "suffering it out" you don't have to sit around your apartment writhing in agony. You can make this passage of time valuable, productive and even enjoyable. Stay busy, meet new people and reinvent yourself!

Step Twelve — What To Do In The Middle Of The Night

What do you do when it's the middle of the night and you have a powerful urge to contact "that man" and your entire support system is asleep?

- Message boards are always available to vent on all night long (examples: the message board on my website www.rhondafindling.com)
- Call supportive friends and acquaintances in different time zones
- Go on dating sites and browse through profiles of men
- Go on Facebook only if you feel strong enough to **NOT GO** on his page. Instead, communicate with people who make you feel safe. Search for people from your past or new people for your future.
- See my list of things to do when and if you are ruminating (Chapter 15)

Step Thirteen — Detaching Is On A Daily Basis

Detaching is a choice and intention made on a daily basis. It's not just one permanent decision. It's the work that's done from hour to hour, minute to minute, second to second. Think of it like you would be working out or taking a shower. You don't just clean yourself one time and that's it. You don't just work out one time at the gym and that's it. You have to do it regularly to see results.

Step Fourteen — Don't Beat Yourself Up!

Don't beat yourself up for having gotten involved with him. It just shows you have the capacity to love. You took a chance, a risk. There's nothing wrong with that. That was then and this is now. The famous Ramm Dass, author of the 60's bestseller *Be Here Now,* says that we have different incarnations in one life so just think of this past relationship as an incarnation — a learning experience. My niece Samantha, who is a collegial athlete, says that softball is a game of errors. Well dating is also a game of errors.You did the best you could under the circumstances and with the knowledge you had then. Of course if you could jump into a time machine and have a do-over, you may have done things differently, but that's because you have lived through it and now have more information. Beating yourself up is self-abusive. Self-hatred. Aggression against yourself. It's a waste of your precious time and energy. It's also a way of trying to control what happened and hoping that there would have been a different outcome. Don't use his hurtful behaviors as an excuse to punish yourself.

Step Fifteen — Be The Woman Who Got Away

In my practice, I've discovered that the women who disappear and move on (even if it's just an act and their hearts are broken) are the ones men often think about and ruminate over. Maybe the loss of you will provoke him to work on himself. Don't show him that you will accept his devaluing, dysfunctional, insulting behavior. Let him miss you. Let him feel your absence. Be the girl who got away. The one who didn't play games or wouldn't take scraps.

The one who wanted more and walked. Then he will never forget you.

Writing Journal

Affirmations:

Today I'll take the high road and maintain. Today I will contain my pain.

I release the thoughts that hold me in my pain.

Writing Exercise:

What did you do or not do to cope with the pain you are struggling with as you work on detaching from "that man".

ELEVEN

Detaching Technologically

Erase All Traces Of Him Technologically

Erase him from your cell phone, phone book and computer.

Facebook

Don't go on your ex Malignant Man's Facebook page! Do not accept his friend requests! Going on his Facebook page or any other socializing sites where he is active is very self-destructive when you're trying to detach from a man. You could see his women Facebook friends, or worse, cutesy messages they scrawl on his wall. You could also read the witty, seductive comments he writes back to them. Why would you give a man, who has rejected or hurt you, the satisfaction of socializing with other women right in front of you?

And God forbid — the worst — the very worst — you could notice on his relationship status is that it says "in a relationship"! Or even more upsetting, what if you see the woman's name and picture whom he's in a relationship with? Then you'll want to become Facebook friends with her to dig up more info on her. You may become insanely angry at her, obsessing all day long over "what does she have that I don't?"

By the time you're done, your whole life will be focused on him and his life. If you don't look, you only have to contend with what you already know. Even if you are a lucky gambler and see that he's still single, just looking at his pictures could upset you or trigger your wanting to contact him. So de-friend him and do not accept any of his friend requests to avoid all of these possible problems.

Take Him Off All Your Socializing Sites

Do not have access to him on any socializing sites.

Get Blocking Software If Necessary

There is software that blocks you from going on websites. There is also software that blocks his incoming calls to you. There is even email software that prevents you from emailing impulsively. It's called *email regret*. Get these software applications if you need them.

Don't Snoopernet Him

Don't go on his blogs, YouTube or Google him! Finding out information on him is destructive. I can't tell you how many people sit on the couch in my office or hysterically cry on the phone when they see that their ex has moved on. Life is difficult enough. Don't look for trouble. Even if you get info on him, then what? There's nothing you can do about it except obsess or talk about it with people in your support system.

And it doesn't end there. You may feel a compulsive need to look him up again to get even more information on him. It is like falling into the rabbit hole. You can't just eat one potato chip. The less you know about him, the better off you are. That's why they say that ignorance is bliss.

Writing Journal

Writing Exercise:

Have you ever snoopernetted your ex? Do you ever look up your ex on Facebook? How can you control yourself from doing these activities?

TWELVE

Why Acting Aggressive Is Not A Good Idea

When a Malignant Man rejects, insults, frustrates, hurts or abandons you, you will experience feelings of aggression. Aggressive feelings and thoughts could lead to aggressive behavior which would be demonstrated by saying or sending emasculating, attacking, degrading, humiliating, insulting texts and/or emails to him; calling and hanging up; hitting, yelling, cursing, following or stalking him. The following are technological aggressive acts:

- Breaking into his email or cell phone accounts
- Writing insulting things on his Facebook wall
- Sabotaging his dating profile(s)
- Sending angry emails or texts to his girlfriend or wife

I strongly suggest not giving into your aggressive impulses, no matter how enraged you are at him. If you aggressively let him have it, it's a momentary release of anger but there's a strong chance it won't lead to him regretting his behavior or choices. In fact, it will probably validate whatever need he had to push you away. You will merely be mirroring his aggressive, hurtful behavior.

Additionally, if you're feeling revengeful and do something vindictive to get even, he'll most likely end up not talking to you. Him completely rejecting you as a result, can lead to further obsessing and wanting to contact him again. Thus the cycle continues.

If there's a part of you that hopes he will ever contact you again for possible reparation, unmercifully attacking him will prevent this from ever happening. In time, he might experience the loss of you as a missed opportunity and feel remorse. He might even regret that he sabotaged the relationship and that you were the "girl who got away".

If you just end things classy, Audrey Hepburn style, who knows? If he emotionally matures and develops psychologically, maybe he'll make a return appearance — more whole and ready for a grownup, healthy, real relationship.

List Of Practical Reasons To Not Act Aggressive With Men You're Angry With

- You may come across as lonely and desperate
- An aggressive enactment will keep you connected to him
- Any of the "good" feelings he had about you will disappear

- He may not own or agree with anything that you say about him
- He'll think you have emotional problems
- There may still be no accountability on his part for his behavior
- It could be more punishing for him to be left thinking he messed up
- You'll end up feeling bad about yourself and erode your self-esteem
- You may not get any relief and then it will be too late
- He may not be responsive to your confrontation
- If you don't contact him you still have power
- He doesn't know you are hurting now but he will know then
- You've made a clean exit with your self-esteem intact and now you'll blow it
- He may not even contact you back, even if you want him too
- If you don't contact him at all he still doesn't know that you care enough to feel angry
- You may say something you will regret later on, which could lead to wanting to apologize to him
- You're back waiting for him to contact you even if your intention was not to get a response
- There is more power in his thinking you don't care

- If you can wait it out and don't have any encounters with him, you will eventually get over your anger at him.

Aggressively Pursuing Men

Some women claim it's hard to accept a man's lack of interest or rejection because they're used to getting everything they want. They're successful financially and in their careers. However, it's a different ball game when it comes to romance. You don't have as much control over one person as you might over a job, project or even money. People's issues about closeness, love, and sexuality is not the same thing as purchasing products or getting promotions.

Don't treat men you are romantically interested in like a business venture. Aggressively pursuing men, who are not reciprocating your level of interest, is not attractive or sexy. It actually comes across as very childish. It just demonstrates that you're mostly into your own thoughts and feelings. You're not taking who he truly is or what he wants, into account.

Do you really want to be in a relationship with a man you have to constantly initiate with and run after? Don't you want to be with someone who's excited about being with you? Even if his lack of enthusiasm is due to pathology, do you still want to be with him? Do you really want to be his therapist?

Bottom line is you can't make a man be or act the way you want. You have to accept where he is emotionally even if you don't like it. Even if you believe he is choosing wrong, ruining a good thing or has issues he needs to work out. Detach. Let him have his free will.

Acting Out Vs. Thinking About

There's a tremendous difference between "acting out" and "thinking" about a man you're getting over.

"Acting out" means taking an action. Contacting him by email, phone, text or going to a place where you know you'll run into him. However, thinking about a man without contacting him is intra psychic work. Your struggle with yourself. It's between you and you, which is a million times better than between you and him.

When you're struggling internally with your feelings, he is not aware of all the emotional work that you're doing and resources you are putting into trying to detach from him. For all he knows, you have completely moved on and don't give him a second thought. This concept can be very empowering.

Handling Your Aggression

It's always better to contain your aggression and anger by working it through rather than acting out. Deal with your anger symbolically, which means expressing your feelings with a therapist, friend, Twelve Step program, creatively, or through physical activity. You can even tell him off to yourself or to a friend standing in for him. Tell him off as if he were really there. Punch a pillow or better yet take up kickboxing. Write an essay or poem about him and read it at an open mic. Write a letter to him and burn it or throw it in the garbage. (See the release ceremony in the last chapter) Sending angry letters to him will only keep the attack defense cycle going, which will drag you deeper into the drama.

Instead, put your energy into diminishing your aggression. This could be done by trying to make time pass productively to forget him and your relationship with him. Try to create new experiences for yourself, to wipe out the old memories of him.

Participate In Energetic Activities To Reduce Your Anger

If you can, try and be more physically active. Sports, exercise, biking, swimming, walking, dancing, running, working out, hiking, doing chores and even laughing can help reduce anger's arousal. The more vigorous the activity, the more effective.

Doing Nothing

I've heard the bestselling author Marianne Williamson say many times in her lectures, based on *The Course In Miracle,* "I need do nothing".

Doing nothing doesn't mean you are a floor mat and a man can just walk all over you. It means you're doing whatever it takes to not try and force things. Just allowing. Accepting what is. Keep in mind that not contacting him is, in itself, a rejection. You're rejecting him. So doing nothing is actually doing something! Do whatever it takes to do nothing.

Instead, release the relationship and its outcome to the universe. The universe has its own intelligence. Take all of your aggressive energy and put it into yourself, your healing and your life.

Writing Journal

Writing Exercise:
What can you do to get yourself to do nothing when you feel a compulsive urge to contact him?

Write a letter to "that man" telling him off for everything he's done to hurt you. Vent all your anger in this letter. Keep writing until you have nothing else to say. You can read it aloud to people in your support system if you like. You can keep the letters for future references or use them in a release ritual (see the last chapter of this book).

Under no circumstances mail this letter to him
Write a letter back from him saying what you think he would say in response to your letter.

Write a letter back from him telling you everything you would need him to say that would give you peace, serenity and closure.

Be grateful to yourself

What makes you grateful about how you've handled your detachment process from him?

Here are some examples:

-I kept my dignity

-It's sad that we never got back together but I'm proud that I never contacted him again

-He doesn't know all the hard work I did to let him go — although he may think I just got over him in a week!

THIRTEEN

Recovery Three To Six Months Later

Don't Go Back For Better Closure

There will always be pain when you're saying good-bye to a man you had a connection with. It will hurt no matter what, even if you say the perfect thing. If you try and fine tune "the end", you're only asking to be re-traumatized, re-hooked and have to start from square one again. Keeping your dignity intact, no longer caring about him or what he thinks, is true closure.

Undoing Pursuing A Man Or Groveling

If you have groveled to a man, you can take your power back by STOPPING. As time passes and he sees you're not pursuing him, he'll only notice your absence. Your clinging will become a distant memory. Immediately reclaim your power by not groveling, pursuing, chasing or initiating contact anymore!

Try Not To Inflate His Importance

Don't put him on a pedestal. As they say in Twelve Step programs, "don't make him your higher power". Once you start heading down that road, immediately make a list of all the negative qualities about him.

Don't Become Friends With Him

Do not be friends with "that man". It is not a sign of maturity or coolness to stay friends with a man who's hurt you. This is not middle school. This is real life. By not staying friends, you are setting a firm boundary. Let him feel the loss of you as a consequence of his behavior and choices.

Reasons Why Your Should Not Stay Friends With Him

- You're only fooling yourself if you think it's not going to upset you when he starts telling you about the other women he's dating.
- You're letting him think it all turned out okay at the end, even if he did hurt or traumatize you.
- It's easier to forget, heal and move on if you aren't reminded of your ex by talking to him and hearing what he's up to.
- You are colluding with his dysfunctional behavior.
- You are showing him you don't feel worthy of your needs.
- Not staying friends will probably increase his opinion of you and your value, even if you never hear from him again.

- If you stay friends, you are putting yourself in a state of frustration and deprivation.

Don't Give Him Satisfaction

My friend Mary told me when I was in my early twenties not to give guys who hurt you satisfaction. It was the best girlfriend advice I ever heard because it's about having pride in yourself. Not giving him the satisfaction of contacting him when he has hurt you will empower you and increase your self-esteem. Don't feed his narcissism.

What If He Keeps Contacting You Even Though You've Set Boundaries?

Even though some Malignant Men won't give you what you need and want — such as commitment, monogamous love, a relationship — some Malignant Men just refuse to be ignored even though they were the ones to reject you. These types of Malignant Men can't see beyond themselves. They don't respect your boundaries. They're just plain selfish and insensitive.

Women, who complain that a Malignant Man just won't stay away, are usually sending double messages. They may even be having sex with him or texting intermittently. If you are determined to get rid of a Malignant Man, consistently set limits and he will leave you alone.

What If A Malignant Man Wants Reparation?

If he wants to repair the severed relationship, you can have specific demands. Here are some suggestions:

- He has to hold himself accountable for hurting you
- He must demonstrate his remorse for hurting you
- He has to want to try to work on having "a relationship" with you, not just friendship
- If he's a Sexually Ambivalent Man, he has to own his romantic feelings and his attraction for you

Letting a man back into your life after he's hurt you is an individual decision. Some women are less forgiving and don't give second chances to men who have threatened their self-respect or hurt them in any way. Letting him back can be risky. If a Malignant Man repeatedly sabotages the relationship then it's probably better to throw in the towel and not take him back.

Sightings

Sometimes we are just not able to be casual when we see a man we are trying to detach from, even if time has passed. Wounds can reopen. Longing can return. You may get traumatized if you see him with a woman.

If you're unfortunate enough to have a sighting of your ex Malignant Man, keep moving. Don't even say hello if you don't feel like it. If you must acknowledge his existence due to social/business circumstances, don't get into a lengthy conversation. Don't make yourself more vulnerable then you have to.

If it helps, pretend that he's a piece of furniture or a tree and walk right past him. This is not being revengeful or playing games. It's just keeping it "real". It's just taking care of yourself.

Psychics

Many women who are trying to detach from relationships with men may want to consult a psychic. Here is my take on psychics; just look at a psychic reading as a source of entertainment. Occasionally psychics can be helpful but many are just narcissistic, claiming they have the answers, can predict the future, psychically spy on people and even read people's minds.

Some psychics will tell you things that are completely false, which could even provoke you to ruminate. For instance, what if they tell you the Malignant Man you are trying to let go of is in a relationship? How would you really know? How do you know they really know? It may provoke you to want to go on Facebook to check out if it's true, which could sabotage all the hard work you did to detach from him.

Keep in mind that doing psychic readings is a way for some people to make quick cash during a bad economy. It's not hard to learn how to read tarot cards. You can just buy them at local or online bookstores.

I would like to add that there are some psychics who are truly intuitive and offer sound spiritual counseling, which can be helpful if they are good at it and their intent to help is genuine.

Continuing No Communication With Him

Keep up your commitment to not calling, emailing, or texting him. Don't slack off now or get loosey-goosey because some time has passed. To ensure your commitment to not communicating with him, here's what you should tell yourself three times a day:

I deserve to be chased. I deserve to be valued. I deserve to be the prize. I deserve to be wanted. I deserve to be married. I deserve to be loved. I deserve to be pursued. I deserve to have a relationship. I deserve to be desired. I do not need to call, email or text that man.

No Communication With That Man Or Snoopernetting Means...

No communication does not necessarily mean that you have completely moved on. No communication does mean that you are not putting up with his hurtful behavior. His destructive defenses. His projections. No communication means that you are taking care of you. You may be falling apart on the inside, but you are doing whatever it takes to show him that you are not pursuing, initiating or running after him.

The following is what "not communicating" with your ex Malignant Man means:

- You have respect for yourself
- You will not tolerate unacceptable behavior from a man who doesn't appreciate you
- You will not pursue a man who does not reciprocate your feelings
- You are putting all your energy into detaching from him
- You are not a masochist
- He's not worthy of your time or attention
- He has hurt you deeply so you won't bother with him anymore
- You are working on you
- You have a lot of things going on in your life and you do not want to deplete your energy
- You do not want to take a chance of getting hurt again
- You don't want to disrupt your life with emotional turmoil

Even if you have not "completely" moved on and he's still renting space in your brain, at least you are taking care of yourself. You're still making progress because your struggle is between you and you now, which is better than between you and him.

Writing Journal

Writing Exercise:

Write out your own game plan describing what you will do if you run into him.

What would you tell a friend to do if her ex tried to make reparation? What would be the criteria you would recommend for her to take him back?

Write a list of what you would like in a relationship with a new man:

Write out the characteristics and traits you would like in a new man. Take the list and put it under your pillow.

Here's a sample list from many of the women clients I have worked with throughout the years:

- *He values me*

- *He appreciates me*

- *He's emotionally mature*

- *He accepts my love*

- *He has the capacity to love back*

- *He's psychologically evolved*

- *He's mentally healthy*

- *He tries to repair the relationship if it's ruptured*

- *He can talk about his own inner life*

- *He can allow himself to be close to me*

- *He is consistent with his feelings about me*

- *He appreciates and values my love*

- *He returns my love with equal adoration and genuine commitment*

- *He loves me and accepts me for who I am*

- *He's kind*

FOURTEEN

Why Do I Still Want To Contact Him?

Sometimes it's maddening that we still think about and long for a Malignant Man even though he has deeply wounded us. Here are some reasons you may still want to contact your ex Malignant Man.

Emotional/Sexual Hunger

You're hungry for love, sex and being touched so it's hard to hold out for a new man. Wanting to be held and connected to a Malignant Man is more powerful than the pain it may cost you.

He's Bringing Up Traumas From Your Past

If you've already been wounded by a parent in your childhood, you may long for the Malignant Man to repair the damage he's incurred, which you unconsciously feel would be healing the original wound from your childhood. You may not be able to remember the pain of the trauma now as an adult but you can feel the original childhood pain from the current trauma with the Malignant Man.

The Rush

You want to get that adrenaline and dopamine rush that makes you feel alive and excited when you see him, hear his voice or read his texts/emails.

You Idealize Him

Just like in the love songs, you're totally crazy about him, no matter how frustrating and hurtful he is. You're afraid you'll never meet anyone who makes you feel the way he does ever again, so it's better to contact him even though you may get hurt and traumatized.

Repetition Compulsion

Sometimes we feel compelled to re-experience certain distressing, early childhood relationships over and over. Repeating our past is irresistible and compulsive. You find yourself in similar, maladaptive and painful situations with men again and again. Freud coined this dynamic repetition compulsion.

The Void

When the Malignant Man is not there anymore you feel a deep void. You'll do anything to not feel the emptiness inside you. Even mental anguish from dealing with him is not so bad as long as you have some connection to him.

Boredom

Lack of challenge at work (or no job) and/or a limited social life can make you want to contact him. You love the drama. It gives you an interesting story to tell.

You Haven't Found Somebody To Replace Him

You've been dating like crazy but can't find anyone to replace him. You're experiencing a lack of available straight, single, divorced, emotionally available men who you can have a viable relationship with. You start to compromise more, overlooking personality traits that you know are dysfunctional.

Anger/Resentment

You keep thinking about how angry he made you. How unfair it is that he treated you the way he did without any consequences. You want another chance to properly tell him off.

You're addicted to longing for him

Rather than be in a real love relationship without games and unhealthy dynamics you are addicted to the state of longing. Prolonged longing can be very romantic (although not very fulfilling) and fuel for great literature and music.

Unfortunately, it's also a way of holding on and not letting go.

Role Modeling

We internalize and copy our mothers, who were involved in relationships and marriages with Malignant Men, and follow in their footsteps.

Denial

You go into denial regarding how much he's hurt you, how disturbed he is, his lack of interest, his inability to commit. Some women don't want to see the truth even when it's staring them right in the face.

Loneliness

The pain of loneliness makes you give Malignant Men more chances even when you see how dysfunctional they are.

"That Man" Is A Bad Habit

Sometimes a woman gets addicted to a person she knows is bad for her. It's as if he is a bad habit that she just can't quit. That's why you have to take it day to day, minute to minute, as if he was a chemical that you are trying not to use anymore.

You're Addicted To Frustration

Some part of you is addicted to the Malignant Man's cat and mouse game. Like a gambler, you're hoping against hope that the repeatedly frustrating Malignant Man will change and you'll have a satisfying relationship.

Writing Journal

Writing Exercise:

Write about any feelings that surface from reading about the 15 possible reasons a woman might want to contact her ex Malignant Man. Do you relate to any of them? If you do, describe them here.

FIFTEEN

Ruminating

Ruminating about your Malignant Man means you are having intrusive thoughts that are usually unwanted, highly stressful and uncomfortable. Ruminating is criticizing, perfecting, editing, reviewing events and conversations that made you angry, hurt or traumatized. They can also be flashbacks, memories, and reflections. You are reliving the event in your mind and reexamining what happened with your Malignant Man. You're going around in a loop again and again without anything changing.

The actual event with the Malignant Man could be locked in the past now but your mind holds onto it. You are reliving the pain of the past even though it's not actually happening in real time. It's dealing with a traumatic memory and not the actual person anymore.

Try To Stop Focusing On His Rejecting Behavior

By dwelling on a rejecting image of "that man" hurting you, you're making yourself feel rejected again as if it were happening in the present. Although it's irresistible to clarify and analyze what happened, it can also be destructive because it chips away at your self-esteem. Additionally, dwelling on a rejecting image gives the Malignant Man power if his intention was to devalue you. You are colluding with his hurtful behavior towards you by repeatedly thinking about how he hurt you, not only that time but over and over again — as many times as you rehearse it in your mind.

What You Tell Yourself May Not Even Be Accurate

You could torture yourself all day long with all sorts of scenarios and stories about your Malignant Man that may not even be true.

By reading the past chapters, you understand that there are a multitude of reasons why he could have hurt you. A Malignant Man could do something that makes sense to him in a moment of fear but makes no sense if he looks back on it later on.

Not having any new "accurate" info on him (because you are heeding my advice to NOT LOOK HIM UP OR GET ANY CURRENT INFO ON HIM), you can make any story up you want about him. Imagine that he's obsessing about you. It might not even be your imagination — it could be true. Just don't think of something that puts you in a painful position! Think of something that empowers you. Think of something that can free you of your past.

Universal Law — Don't Look Back!

"Not looking back" is a subject written about throughout the Bible. One of the most famous stories in the Old Testament is when Lot's wife turns into a pillar of salt as she looks back at the city Sodom and Gomorrah crumbling, while she and her family are running away.

Spiritually our path is to ascend, not go backwards. If you do go back by contacting him or looking him up, you may have to end up pulling yourself out of the abyss that you have worked so hard to climb out of.

Writing Journal

Writing Exercise:

Do you ever find yourself ruminating? If you do, what usually triggers your ruminating? How do you stop yourself?

SIXTEEN

Destructive Thoughts That Disempower You

Often women, who are detaching from a Malignant Man, think self-negating disempowering thoughts. Some of these thoughts are completely your own and have absolutely nothing to do with the reality of what he's thinking. Your thoughts could even be projections of your own self-hatred, stemming from childhood traumas or from the media. Here are some examples of self-negating and negative thoughts I'm referring to:

- He's more desirable than me
- Other women are more attractive and appealing than me
- There's a scarcity of men out there
- I'll never find anyone as wonderful as him
- He was the great love of my life
- I'll never meet anyone as good as him
- I'll be alone forever
- I'm not enough for him
- I'm not good-looking enough for him
- I'm inadequate as a woman
- I'm not as desirable as other women

It would be helpful to your detachment process to replace negative thoughts with constructive thoughts. Here are some sample things to think instead:

Constructive Things To Think:

- He is just one person among many
- He is just one bad experience
- He may be suffering too
- It may have been an empty win for him
- There may have been major consequences for him as well
- He may have longed for me too but couldn't act on it
- He regrets the way he acted towards me
- He may have lost the best friend he ever had
- He may have lost the best sex he's ever had
- He feels like he lost a great opportunity
- He regrets he couldn't tell you what his real problem was
- He regrets the loss of me
- He ended up with no love or intimacy
- He feels lonely and isolated
- He may be doing to other women what he's done to me
- He feels like a failure because he can't have a relationship like other men involved in long-term relationships

- The best is yet to come
- It's time to start writing a new chapter
- That was then this is now
- It's time to reinvent myself
- The party's not over yet
- What's next?
- It's better to be alone than with a man who doesn't value me
- It's better to be healthy alone than sick with someone else
- I will heal, and so it is
- He may be like a movie star to me but to others he's irrelevant and mediocre
- He is just one small piece of my life
- Be patient and see how things unfold
- I need to move on and start living my life again because I won't live forever
- See who shows up
- Perhaps this relationship wasn't for my highest good
- The love of my life is out there and now the path is ready for us to meet

Reasons You Enjoy The Time You Have Being Single

- You can flirt with whom you want
- You can fall in love again
- You can spend your money the way you want
- You can come and go as you want

Surrender To "What Is"

Alexander Graham Bell was believed to have said, "When one door closes, another opens; but we often look so long and so regretfully upon the closed door that we do not see the ones which open for us". Who knows what you were spared?

Writing Journal

Writing Exercise:
Make your own list of what's good about being single and unattached
Make a list of "that man's" negative qualities
Make your own list of positive thoughts to replace destructive thoughts you may have
Write in your journal about what you were possibly spared by not being in a relationship with your ex

Creating a new future

Make a list of your goals for your new future without him. This is where you are going to put your life force energy.

Here are some affirmations of letting go of "that man" and moving on:

- *I have a chance for a brand new and better beginning*

- *I feel so good being free of him and all the pain connected to him*

- *I move on and feel a sense of excitement to let this old part of my life go*

- *I have other things in store for me that I am now able to connect to*

SEVENTEEN

How To Stop Ruminating And Thinking Destructive Thoughts

Here are actions you can take to stop yourself when you are in the throws of ruminating or having self-destructive thoughts. Use your journal to jot down ideas and thoughts that come up for you as you read.

Distract Yourself

The moment you find yourself thinking about him, try and redirect your attention somewhere else. For instance, I think about traveling when I am purposely trying to not think about the past or ruminate — a trip I want to make, even if it's years from now. I'd go on the internet and research out the entire trip including possible hotels, things to do, etc. Put on a DVD or TV show that captivates you. There's no way you can watch "Locked Up Abroad" and obsess about a man at the same time.

Find Activities/Interests That Absorb Your Attention

During this time period, you need to find absorbing activities and interests that capture your attention. Another man, your career, travel, a creative project, returning to school, a sport, etc.

Be Mindful

Bring your thoughts into the present moment. Be mindful
   of your body, your
surroundings. Where are you? What does the room smell
   like? What does the page
you're reading feel like if you touch it? What are your
   surroundings? Describe them.
What are you doing now? What joy can you find in what is
happening right now? Being in the moment can reduce
suffering and deepen the pleasure and happiness of being
alive.

Think About Your "Time"

How much "time" do you want to spend thinking and
talking about what happened with "that man"? Is this how
you want to spend the precious "time" you have left on this
earth? Wouldn't you rather enjoy the life you have now,
even if it doesn't include him?

Meaning

We can extrapolate meaning from all of our experiences.
Studies have shown that resilient people in horrifying
circumstances survived by finding meaning in what
happened to them. So try to focus on the "gift" you got
from your experience with "that man". The next time you
are ruminating or angry, ask yourself what you learned

from the experience with "that man"? What meaning did it have for you? How is your life different from having known him?

Focus On What Can Be Rather Than What Is

Stop putting so much focus on the upsetting incident that occurred or the relationship that ended. This situation is not permanently glued to you. Think of things in life you want in place of ruminating about him. Goals, dreams, new experiences, new people, new men.

Process Your Feelings With People (Not Him)

Call a supportive, nonjudgmental, empathic friend and talk through your feelings. Call another friend afterwards if you still need to talk. You can stay on the phone all night long processing, just as long as you don't contact "that man".

Cry

If you need to, let yourself CRY! It will make you feel better and often stops the obsessing. Crying is the body's mechanism for expressing grief. When you cry your feelings move through you. Afterwards you may feel better. It's especially healing to cry with someone there as you process your pain (not "that man" though).

Take An Action (Not An Action To Contact Him)

It's hard to ruminate and be active at the same time. Start doing something that has nothing to do with "that man". Watch TV or a DVD, clean your house, volunteer to baby-sit for an overwhelmed mother. Just get out of the house and get fresh air and sunlight. Look at photos from your past when times were better (not of "that man" though). Physical exercise helps a lot. Work out, run, walk or play a sport. Even walk around the mall — I'm not advocating retail therapy but it's distracting if you're in the throes of wanting to contact him or obsessing about him. Just do something. See the list of suggested things to do at the end of this chapter.

Make a Gratitude List

Make a list of things you are grateful about right now. Here's a sample of things you can appreciate right now:

- You are alive and breathing
- You have enough money to buy this book
- You have the ability to see and read this book

Sublimate/Transmute Your Pain

Use your creativity to transmute the pain you're in to something positive and productive. Write a poem, story or a song about the situation. Do something constructive with the adversity.

I was going through a breakup back in the 90's. I wrote *Don't Call That Man!* as a way to work through my own feelings of anguish and loss over a relationship that didn't work out. As a result I got published, which led to my building a successful private practice and leaving my job at a mental health clinic. Looking back, that was a much better prize than the man who, I realize now, was dysfunctional and emotionally unavailable.

Meditate

There's lots of scientific evidence that meditation helps people mentally and physically, even if it's for only a few minutes a day. If you've never meditated before there are plenty of CDs out there that will help you. Deepak Chopra's meditation tapes are my favorite. I went to one of his workshops and it was fantastic!

Do Or Think About Something That Makes You Happy

Instead of thinking about "that man" focus on things that make you happy. Here are some examples: Knowing that you're going out to have brunch with a good friend you haven't seen in awhile. Trick or treating with your children or nieces and nephews. Eating pumpkin pie at Thanksgiving dinner with your family. Going to the beach in the summer or the winter when you go to a tropical island.

Now make your own list in your journal.

Suggested Things To Do Immediately When You Are Obsessing

I know this may sound difficult but I highly suggest you do not take your cell phone with you if you leave the house when you do any of the suggested activities, so you are not tempted to call or text "that man".

Go to a bookstore and just read
Eat chocolate
Drink a cup of coffee
Have a cup of tea
Take a shower
Shampoo your hair
Get a new hairstyle
Color your hair or change the color
Go to a salon and get your hair shampooed and blown out
Take a bath by candlelight
Snap a rubber band or pinch yourself
Go swimming
Go to a karaoke place and sing a great song
Ask for a hug (but not from "that man")
Watch a sunset
Watch a sunrise
Go hiking
Plan a trip
Chant

Go to a casino and play Black Jack

Have a glass of wine

Go to a bar and have a beer

Go on dates (even blind dates from dating sites— they're distracting!)

Go to a café and eat a dessert

Figure out how to make more money

Go to a movie

Go to a Broadway musical

Get a massage

Get a facial

Write to men who contacted you through dating sites but whom you never responded to

Write a letter to the Malignant Man but don't send it

Write a poem

Go to an open mic

Go to a comedy club

Groom

Pluck your eyebrows

Paint

Go work out in a gym

Catch up on current events

Go to a mall and people -watch

Go to a park and sit on a bench and eat an ice cream cone

Go to a makeup counter and have them give you a makeover

Go to a ball game

Talk to someone in your support system

Go see a scary movie

Throw yourself into your work

Eat some comfort food (if you're not on a diet)

Take part in a sport

Get a manicure

Give yourself a manicure or pedicure

Take a day trip

Go to a neighborhood near you that you haven't been to yet

Pay bills

Lie in the sun

Ask out a new man you've been eying

Organize something in your apartment

Clean out your closet

Organize your papers

Go through your old photos

Work on a scrapbook

Go through your old clothes

Do something in nature

Listen to CD's and DVD's of famous motivators and spiritual people

Have sex — with yourself or someone else other than "that man"

Clean your house or a part of your house

Surf the internet

Build your own website

Start a blog of your own

Dust

Balance your checkbook

Organize your desk

Visualize a mental picture of your perfect relationship

Make a list of people who love you

Take a short day trip

Plan a party

Go on a trip out of town that weekend (if you can afford this)

Go some place new in your area

Go to a singing bar

Listen to someone else's problems

Call your therapist

Find a therapist

Make a list of goals

Hang out with a person/people you love/like

Make a list of your accomplishments

Go to a Twelve Step program meeting

Call into a Twelve Step program phone group

Go to a bookstore

Take yourself out on a date

Take yourself out to dinner

Pray

Talk to a clergy member

Try to make yourself laugh

Take a nap

Go to a church or temple

Take a shower

Play with a child

Play with a pet

Go to a pet store

Go to an art gallery

Go to an art museum

Read

Go to a DVD store and get out a good movie

Watch TV

Garden

Plant seeds for new flowers or tulips bulb for next season

Read affirmations

Go to the beach

Go for a drive

Start a scrapbook

Go bowling

Make your own video and put it on youtube

Host your own radio show

Long-Term Things To Do To Control Ruminating

Volunteer — help people less fortunate than you. Giving distracts you from yourself.

Plan a trip — when you have things to look forward to they help you to not obsess because you're focused on the new and exciting things coming up in your life.

Plan on taking a course — something you've wanted to study for a long time. It can be just for pleasure, a way to meet a new circle of people, something to help you earn money or advance your career.

Work harder on your career — throwing yourself into your work can help, plus you have the rewards of more money or a big promotion.

Build your support system

Here's a sample of some things you can do to meet more people:

- Take a class
- Join an organization
- Do volunteer work
- Get in touch with relatives and old friends you haven't heard from in a while
- Go to your local pub and socialize
- Go to a meetup.com meeting or start your own
- Throw a party and use it as an excuse to invite new people. Have friends invite friends you've never met to the party
- Make a commitment to go out at least twice a week to a place where you can meet people
- Participate in groups, events and social occasions where people have the same interests as you
- Twelve Step program phone groups encourage people to exchange phone numbers

Notes To Yourself

Put stickers up all over your house with positive slogans and affirmations.

Example:

"Choose me" "Choose now" "Focus on my life" "Don't call that man" "Don't text that man"

Psychotherapy

If, after all these suggestions, you are still thinking about "that man" excessively, I suggest seeking out professional help. Going to a skilled psychotherapist can be enormously helpful and the missing ingredient in your healing process. Medication can also be helpful when obsessing is overwhelming.

Writing Journal

Writing Exercise:

Make your own list of things to do to not obsess
Here are some questions to ask yourself to help jump-start creative ideas.

- *Is there anything you have always imagined doing that you've never done before?*
- *What have you done in the past that you enjoyed?*
- *What could you do alone that you enjoy?*
- *What could you do with other people that you enjoy?*
- *What have you observed that other people do for entertainment and pleasure?*

- *What can you do that can be easily fitted into the spare time of your day?*
- *What can you do that costs money?*
- *What can you do that is free?*
- *What can you do outdoors?*
- *What can you do at home?*

EIGHTEEN

Six Months Later To One Year Later The Healing Journey Continues

How Long Does It Take To Get Over "That Man"?

Detaching isn't a linear process. You will get pockets of time when you start to totally forget about him. Then, out of nowhere, he's back in your thoughts. You're overwhelmed by a memory or longing to speak to him. Sometimes we heal in percentages. For instance, over a year it may be 50% recovery and before you know it you're 75% recovered.

If you experienced abuse, abandonment or rejection in your childhood, healing could take you longer, because it may trigger trauma from your past. You simply can't put a date on when you'll be completely over him. Everyone has a different time frame.

Don't let anyone judge how long it takes you. This is your journey. There's no "getting over that man" police! If anybody tells you "you should be over him by now", even though you were doing the hard work of not contacting him, don't go to that person for support anymore.

Dealing With Loneliness

Often women will want to contact an ex Malignant Man because of sheer loneliness. However, going back to a Malignant Man who hurts you is not the solution. The reality is there are many married folks who are lonely too. Women in unhappy marriages will tell you that it is worse to be lonely when you're in a relationship because, at least, when you're alone you have the possibility and hope of meeting someone new. Remember, it's better to be healthy alone than sick with someone else.

So if you're feeling lonely, instead of reaching out to your ex Malignant Man, think of ways to fill your life up. Hobbies, interests, passions. Bringing more people into your life. Bring more love into your life. Not necessarily romantic love. Learn how to nurture and soothe yourself.

Learn to endure loneliness. It's a part of life. Sometimes just feeling the loneliness and moving through it is enough. This too shall pass. It always does.

Meeting New Men

Meeting lots of new men will certainly distract you in your detachment process. Some women have the ability to meet new men right away because they know a lot of people who will introduce them. Working in a place where there are lots of men certainly helps.

We often hear how quickly women celebrities find new boyfriends after going through a breakup, but that's probably because they're always going to events and parties. They're exposed to new people all the time. If they want to meet a particular man, they can just get "their people" (publicists) to call "his people".

If you're very "picky" it may take you longer. I've had some women clients who found it easier to find a new relationship because they were attracted to a large variety of men. They didn't have a type.

Individuation

Meeting a new man is not the only solution for detaching from your ex. You can use this time to grow emotionally and finally work through ancient attachments from your past. This can also be an opportunity for transformation and to explore your interests and passions. Some women go back to school or start new careers. Others follow a dream they had put on hold. You can utilize this time to reinvent yourself.

The Length Of Time To Get Over A Man Depends On:

- What he meant to you
- How deeply in love you were
- How deeply he hurt you
- How attached to him you were
- How many people you have in common in your life
- How often you have to see him

- How destructive his projections onto you were
- How many men you meet
- Meeting someone new
- How involved you are with other parts of your life
- How busy you are
- How good you are at mourning and grieving and working through
- How much love you have in your life
- How selective you are
- How committed you are to not contacting him
- If he is in your life (your coworker or father of your children)
- Past adult traumas you've had
- Past childhood traumas you've had
- If he reminded you of one of your parents you had a traumatic relationship with
- Your connection and involvement with other parts of your life (work, interests, hobbies, family, friends)
- Your ability to be alone
- Your resiliency
- How you use this time

Do Not Give Into Curiosity

After all this time, continue to not look him up! Curiosity doesn't mean you have to satisfy the craving. The info doesn't really serve any purpose. It's only perpetuating your attachment and connection to him. You might get hurt. It could take you even more time to recover. Keep focusing on your life and detaching from him. It takes will power but you can do it. Endure your curiosity. Remember that "curiosity killed the cat".

Accept Yourself For Where You Are

Don't listen to people who tell you that you can hang out with him now that some time has passed. If you still need to stay away from him, then stay away.

In fact, you don't have to say hello if you run into him, even if two years have passed. Even if three years have passed. Taking care of your "self" is the priority. Self-preservation, self-repair, self-esteem and self-respect are the operant words here.

Bad Dates

Try to keep dating other men unless you absolutely hate it. Dating can be distracting and add stories to your life that are different from "the story" about "that man".

Bad dates are not an excuse to contact your ex Malignant Man. Just because you're not meeting "the one" or your "soul mate" doesn't warrant a slip backwards. If you're upset about a "bad date" call someone in your support system to express your disappointment or frustration. Don't call, email or text "that man!" to undo feeling upset about a "bad date".

Don't Test Yourself To See If You're Ready To See Him

Now that some time has passed, don't walk around his neighborhood or talk to his friends to see if it still bothers you. Don't go on his Facebook page now to check out any of his new women friends or his relationship status. Keep up no contact and no snoopernetting.

Sometimes You Have To Live With The Questions

Looking back, you may never understand why things turned out the way they did. Why he acted a certain way. Why he hurt you; why he left; why he's ambivalent; why he was cold and rejecting when he told you he liked you so much.

As the famous poet Rilke said, "Sometimes we have to live with the questions". Besides, there are no guarantees that if you had the answers, they would help you anyway. If you try and get the answers by contacting him or snooping around, all the healing and hard work you did will be wiped out and you'll have to start all over again. So learn to live with the unknown.

Stop Telling "Your Story" Of What Happened With Him To New People

Since you've pretty much processed your feelings at this point, try and cut down on telling "your story" about him to new people that you meet. Every time you tell the saga about what happened with you and "that man", you give power to the story. You can also retraumatize yourself by reliving what happened.

So, unless you meet someone you are completely sure will enlighten you with insightful clarification such as a brand new therapist (or running into Deepak Chopra or Oprah), try to stop telling new people the "story".

Forgetting

A lot of the healing work will be trying to forget "that man". The more you forget, the easier it is to no longer feel the pain of what happened. It gets to the point that you literally can't remember being angry with him or loving him anymore. That's why I highly suggest to try and create new memories to layer over your past memories of "that man".

Here's my "apple juice theory". Suppose you are holding a glass of apple juice that would represent your bad memories. Imagine pouring water from the faucet, which would represent happy experiences, into the glass of apple juice. Eventually the water would dilute the apple juice. That's how it is with good and bad experiences. If you keep creating new memories that have nothing to do with him, the positive memories will eventually outweigh the bad memories.

Another important part of the 'forgetting" process is not bringing more trauma from "that man" into your life. Not having contact with him or learning new information about him makes forgetting so much easier.

Because time does heal all wounds, your memory of him will eventually fade. The memory traces in your brain actually start to erode. That's why they say that time heals all wounds. Think of forgetting "that man" as a melting popsicle.

Mistakes

Mistakes are unavoidable. They're part of being human. When you are aware of mistakes you made, let them go. If you are still upset over any mistakes you made in your relationship with "that man", even the choice of getting involved with him, here's an exercise you can do.

Go back in time when the "mistake" was made, including the decision to get involved with him. Try to remember what you were thinking and feeling right before you made the choice you think could have been a mistake. Did you consider the outcome that upset you or did you hope for it to turn out better? Did you have any idea of the pain that you would feel? Try to remember the need or needs that pushed you into making the decision. Recall the strength of those needs and how they influenced your choice. Maybe if you get back in touch with exactly how you felt, then you'd understand why you made the decision that you now consider a "mistake".

Forgive yourself for your mistakes

If you keep beating yourself up for your mistakes, you are being sadistic to yourself. So you must try and stop it.

You already have paid for your mistake. You have endured those consequences and felt the pain.

You made the only decision you could make, given the needs and awareness at the moment you made it.

Here's an affirmation for self-forgiveness:

I forgive myself and accept myself just the way I am and love myself unconditionally just the way I am in all my power and magnificence.

What If I'm Still Angry At Him After All This Time?

Don't be upset if you're still sitting on a lot of anger. You just need more time. There could be past traumas from your childhood or adolescence that are at the root of your anger. It might be helpful to see a therapist to help you work through your anger, especially if it's around past issues. You will eventually get over your anger because time passes and there are other opportunities and events in life that will cause the anger to subside. And as the cliché goes "time heals all wounds" so try to "ride the anger out" without "acting it out".

In the event you have any urges to tell him off, here reasons not to:

- Maybe he's going for professional psychological help and was going to eventually apologize but now he never will
- To get even he may tell you he's met someone else even if it's not true
- It's just not worth the gamble of the hurt and pain you may have to go through again
- You're giving him gratification of knowing that he can continue to push your buttons after all of this time
- You'll look like you're still holding on to him
- You won't feel any relief from telling him off
- You've opened the door for him to be back in your life without any growth on his part so nothing has changed
- If you ended the relationship, you hold the power because you denied him "you" because of the way he treated you

Writing Journal

Writing Exercise:

What can I do to work through my anger without contacting my ex?

NINETEEN

Closure

Releasing His Projections

Whatever a Malignant Man has projected onto you needs to be reversed. Here is a writing exercise to accomplish this task. Take your journal and thoughtfully fill out the questions. Don't do this quickly. Really take your time.

Make a list of negative feelings about yourself he elicited from you

e.g.: Shaky self-esteem? I'm not as attractive as other women.

Now say out loud:

"None of this is true. I was owning your projections due my own issues and insecurities. I don't buy what you said."

Now tear up the list and say out loud:

"I recognize what you did was from your own selfishness and self-protection. But your behavior is unacceptable to me and I will never put myself in this position again."

Now write in your journal what you are taking back from what he has taken from you. Here's a sample of things I have heard some women claim they took back from men who have hurt them:

- Their adoration
- Their devotion
- Their sexiness
- Their beauty
- Their attention
- Their interest in him
- Their time
- Their energy
- Their intelligence
- Their wisdom

What Are The Good Things About You That He Deprived Himself Of?

List all the "great" things about yourself he lost out on. Here are some examples:

- My great sense of humor
- My love

- My worldliness

- My listening to him

What Are You Grateful To Him About What He Added To Your Life?

This is a hard one. If you are not ready for this writing exercise, go back to it later. Here are some samples of what women have shared with me throughout the years:

- He helped me out financially

- He made me feel loved

- He made me feel beautiful

- He helped me with my career

- He made me feel interesting

- He was a good father to my children

Release Ceremony

Working with metaphors, symbols and images can sometimes be very healing when working though trauma. Often trauma is stored in the brain in places we can't even reach through talking, so ceremonial or ritual letting go can also be helpful in obtaining closure and transformation.

The following are release ceremonies that can be very helpful in the process of letting go. I have actually done these ceremonies in Arizona. It's better if you do these rituals with someone for support and witnessing:

Write Out The "Story"

Write out the "story" of what happened between you and him. It can be handwritten or typed on the computer.

Pictures Of Him

Pick out three pictures of him.

Tear Up The "Story"

Tear up the written "story" of what happened between the two of you. Divide it into three piles.

Throw Them Somewhere

Go to a place where you decide to throw away one photo of him and one pile of the torn "story". When you get there, tear up one of the pictures.
I once threw an ex boyfriend's picture into the Grand Canyon!
I've known women to throw them in the garbage outside of Denny's. I think the Grand Canyon is much more dramatic.

Throw Them In Fire

Tear up the second picture; throw it and the second part of the "story" into a fire to burn them up.

Fire has always been the element of transformation. Something powerful happens when you see your words turn into ashes and rise up in smoke, or see a picture of your ex curling up from the sides. It's almost like you're in a 1940's Betty Davis movie when she'd throw a love letter into the fire and watch it burn.

Throw Them In Water

Tear up the last picture of him and third pile of the written "story" and throw it into water — a creek, river or the ocean. Let a fast stream of water or a wave from the ocean take it away. Water possesses healing and cleansing qualities.

I once watched an ex-boyfriend's (the same one from the Grand Canyon) torn-up picture floating down a creek, on a vortex, in Sedona. It was very gratifying.

Use Your Own Imagination Of A Ceremony To Release And Let Go Of "That Man"

What symbolic ceremony and ritual could you do that would help you in your healing process of your "ex"?

Different Healing Modalities

Although I strongly advise psychotherapy to work though trauma and loss, I've found that different types of healing modalities can also help. Here are ways some women have found healing for a relationship that ended:

- Looking at art
- Travel
- Massage
- Meditation
- Prayer
- Workshops
- Listening to spiritual DVD's (Deepak Chopra, Esther Hicks/Abraham, etc.)
- Dance
- Journaling
- Creativity
- Work
- Beauty Treatments (a makeover, a new hairdo, manicure/pedicure)
- Reiki
- Exercise

Writing Journal

Writing Exercise:
What activities or treatments have you found healing for you?

TWENTY

Forgiving "That Man"

To forgive a man who's deeply hurt you is one of the most difficult challenges you may ever experience. You deserve a medal after you've successfully done this emotional work.

Sometimes, if you're lucky, you can even get to a place where you truly understand that his wounding you was probably due to issues he struggles with. That's not an excuse to tolerate his mistreatment of you but, at least, you can stop personalizing his behavior and let go of your anger. Your enlightenment doesn't mean that you ever have to talk to "that man" again if you don't want to.

I personally think that forgiving your ex means that you are no longer focused on how he hurt you. Your deep wound has healed and it's just a scab.

When you do forgive him, you've made a monumental developmental achievement and moved up a notch psychologically. There's an interpersonal maturity that is developed during this process of inner struggle with pain, joy and loss. So you have not only survived, you have triumphed. Be proud.

The best part is "he" has no idea of all the hard work you went through and he never has to know. It's really none of his business.

When you have finally met the challenge of detaching from "that man" STILL try to continue not to email, text, Facebook, call or look "that man" up on the internet.

The memory of the electrifying rush of connecting with "that man" may still haunt you, but there's something to be said for peace, serenity, sanity, productivity and having the emotional availability for a new man.

There is more to life than your ex Malignant Man. A world filled with rich and unknown possibilities. A world of potential new relationships, new connections and new ways of expanding yourself. So keep working on "you" and rejoice that you are finally, finally free.

ABOUT THE AUTHOR

Rhonda Findling is a psychotherapist and author of the acclaimed *Don't Call That Man! A Survival Guide To Letting Go, The Commitment Cure: What To Do When You Fall For An Ambivalent Man, The Dating Cure, A Jewish American Princess Dethroned* and *Portrait of My Desire*. Rhonda has appeared on national talk shows including CNN Headline News, Ricki Lake, Geraldo, Maury Povitch, Eye Witness News, Good Day New York, Carnie, Ilyana, Tempest and Judith Regan Tonight. She has led workshops and seminars in New York, L.A., Paris, Berlin and London. Rhonda has been featured in the New York Post, Los Angeles Times, The Boston Globe, Newsday, Rocky Mountain News, Cosmopolitan magazine, Latina Magazine, Glamour (UK and Paris editions) Le Progress, Life and Style, US Weekly, Femina and Today"s Black Woman.

She can be contacted at www.rhondafindling.com

Printed in Great Britain
by Amazon